ORTHO'S All About

Storage Solutions

Project Editor: Paul Ehrlich
Writers: Dave Toht and Jim Sanders
Illustrators: Jeff Anderson, Dave Brandon, and Mario Ferro

Meredith® Books
Des Moines, Iowa

Ortho® Books
An imprint of Meredith® Books

Ortho's All About Storage Solutions
Solaris Book Development Team
Publisher: Robert B. Loperena
Editorial Director: Christine Jordan
Managing Editor: Sally W. Smith
Acquisitions Editors: Robert J. Beckstrom,
    Michael D. Smith
Publisher's Assistant: Joni Christiansen
Graphics Coordinator: Sally J. French
Editorial Coordinator: Cass Dempsey
Production Manager: Linda Bouchard

Meredith Book Development Team
Project Editor: Larry Erickson
Art Director: Tom Wegner
Copy Chief: Catherine Hamrick
Copy and Production Editor: Terri Fredrickson
Contributing Copy Editor: Jay Lamar
Contributing Proofreaders: Todd Keith, Steve Hallam
Electronic Production Coordinator: Paula Forest
Editorial and Design Assistants: Kathleen Stevens, Judy
    Bailey, Kaye Chabot, Treesa Landry, Karen Schirm
Production Director: Douglas M. Johnston
Production Manager: Pam Kvitne
Assistant Prepress Manager: Marjorie J. Schenkelberg
Electronic Production Coordinator: Paula Forest

**Additional editorial contributions from
    Art Rep Services**
Director: Chip Nadeau
Designer: lk Design
Illustrators: Jeff Anderson and Dave Brandon

Meredith® Books
Editor in Chief: James D. Blume
Design Director: Matt Strelecki
Managing Editor: Gregory H. Kayko
Executive Ortho Editor: Benjamin W. Allen

Director, Sales & Marketing, Retail: Michael A. Peterson
Director, Sales & Marketing, Special Markets:
    Rita McMullen
Director, Sales & Marketing, Home & Garden Center
    Channel: Ray Wolf
Director, Operations: George A. Susral

Vice President, General Manager: Jamie L. Martin

Meredith Publishing Group
President, Publishing Group: Christopher M. Little
Vice President, Consumer Marketing & Development:
    Hal Oringer

Meredith Corporation
Chairman and Chief Executive Officer: William T. Kerr

Chairman of the Executive Committee: E.T. Meredith III

Photographers
King Au: 36L, 71T, 78B
Laurie Black: 74T, 74M, 91
Ernest Braun Photography: 28BL, 54T
Ross Chapple Photography: 6B
Chuck Crandall/Crandall & Crandall: 79B
Stephen Cridland: 28BR
Edward Gohlich Photography: 54BL, 54BR, 62MR, 62BR,
    66BL, 71B
Jim Hedrich: 41T
Hedrich-Blessing Studios: 10T
Bill Holt: 10M, 63BL
Bill Hopkins Jr.: 78T, 88
William Hopkins Sr.: cover, 27L, 73T
Roy Inman: 26
Jon Jensen: 27R, 40B, 46B, 60R, 64, 66T
Mike Jensen: 25B, 60L, 74B
Gene Johnson: 66BR
Jenifer Jordan: 24T, 52, 62TR
Scott Little: 4
Barbara Martin: 41M, 70
Beth Singer: 58B
William Stites Photography: 37TL
Rick Taylor Photography: 25T, 28T, 30TL, 30TR, 46M, 59,
    73B, 82T, 82B, 83
Jessie Walker: 10B, 36R, 84T, 84B
James Yochum: 6T, 7B, 24B, 58T

All of us at Ortho® Books are dedicated to providing you
with the information and ideas you need to enhance your
home and garden. We welcome your comments and
suggestions about this book. Write to us at:
Meredith Corporation
Ortho Books
1716 Locust St.
Des Moines, IA 50309–3023

If you would like more information on other Ortho
products, call 800-225-2883 or visit us at www.ortho.com

Note to the Readers: Due to differing conditions, tools,
and individual skills, Meredith Corporation assumes no
responsibility for any damages, injuries suffered, or losses
incurred as a result of following the information published
in this book. Before beginning any project, review the
instructions carefully, and if any doubts or questions remain,
consult local experts or authorities. Because codes and
regulations vary greatly, you always should check with
authorities to ensure that your project complies with all
applicable local codes and regulations. Always read and
observe all of the safety precautions provided by
manufacturers of any tools, equipment, or supplies,
and follow all accepted safety procedures.

STORAGE BASICS — 4

Analyzing the Problem — 6
Planning Effective Solutions — 8
Storage from Stores — 11
Basic Techniques — 12
Materials for Storage Projects — 13
Basic Tools for Building Your Storage Solutions — 14
Building Basic Units — 16

KITCHENS, BATHROOMS, LAUNDRY AND UTILITY ROOMS — 24

The Kitchen — 26
Bathrooms — 36
Laundry and Utility Rooms — 40

BEDROOMS AND CLOSETS — 44

Making Effective Use of Bedroom Walls — 46
Taming the Closet — 47
Seasonal Storage Options — 52
Lining a Closet with Aromatic Cedar — 53
Storage Solutions in Children's Rooms — 54

LIVING AND WORKING AREAS — 58

Entries and Hallways — 60
Formal Living Rooms — 62
Family Rooms and Great Rooms — 64
Dining Rooms — 66
Home Offices — 70
Workshops and Hobby Centers — 73

ATTIC, BASEMENT, GARAGE, AND YARD SOLUTIONS — 78

Unfinished Attic Solutions — 80
Finished Attic Solutions — 82
Basement Solutions — 84
Building Rough-and-Ready Adjustable Utility Shelves — 86
Building a Wine Rack — 87
Attacking Garage Gridlock — 88
Climbing the Walls — 90
Buying Solutions — 91
Storage Solutions in Your Yard — 92
Building a Storage Shed — 93

Glossary — 96
Metric Conversions — 96

*Storage options must be tailored to individual needs and style.
This formal living room demands an elegant wall storage system.
It serves mainly as a display case yet holds a television set that
can be concealed when not in use.*

STORAGE BASICS

IN THIS SECTION

Analyzing the Problem **6**
Planning Effective
Solutions **8**
Storage from Stores **11**
Basic Techniques **12**
Materials for
Storage Projects **13**
Building Basic Units **16**

Whether you own or rent the space you call home, you probably wish it were bigger. That's a common lament: There just isn't enough room for everything. And who has the strength of character—or a strong enough back—to solve the problem by hauling armloads of stuff to the nearest dumpster?

Well, relax. You have more alternatives than living in clutter or throwing out treasures. And you have help: With this book, you can learn to make efficient use of the space you already have and create new storage areas.

The goal of a good storage plan is to keep items safe, secure, and readily available when you need them. Achieving this goal requires more than a few storage bins and some shelves. Implementing a storage plan involves organizing your space and your belongings.

This chapter will get you started with some planning tips, plus instructions to build the basics units of storage systems.

Later chapters take you through specific areas around your home: the kitchen, bath, and laundry and utility rooms; bedrooms and closets; living and working spaces; then attics, basements, garages, and your yard. Each chapter begins with ideas you can use to develop storage solutions then guides you through do-it-yourself projects designed to get "stuff" under control.

ANALYZING THE PROBLEM

Most older homes lack adequate storage space, partly because it rarely was a design priority. Architects today think more about storage. But even when a house has plenty of space, using it to your best advantage requires good planning.

DEALING WITH MORE AND MORE

Over the years, all of us tend to accumulate possessions. One moving company estimates that the average household grows by 1,000 pounds of property per year. Households expand even if the size of the living space does not. Babies need diapers, high chairs, strollers. Then children grow out of clothing and toys. Your own interests bring new items into your life: an expanding library, collectibles, computer accessories, and equipment for cooking, hobbies, and sports.

Storage is needed for appliances you don't want to live without: A food processor, computer, audio and video equipment all demand space to store them as well as room to enjoy them. Time adds not only to the list of cherished mementoes we keep but also to the mass of household records.

*In attacking your storage problems, assess what belongs where and how your family uses each room. You can find good storage space around a room's fixed points of interest—the window, **above,** and the fireplace, **below.***

GETTING STARTED ON SOLUTIONS

Your approach to storage will be unique to your home and needs. No rules apply to every situation. If you're a renter, for example, you probably will need to use freestanding storage devices rather than built-ins. But certain techniques can help you solve even the toughest storage problems.

Effective storage solutions arise when living patterns are compatible with a home rather than at cross-purposes. For example, if furniture blocks easy access to a storage area, putting away or retrieving items can be awkward, making the storage area little used. Such conflicting uses of space undermine attempts to improve storage.

BE SYSTEMATIC: Solving storage problems requires being logical and organized. But you can approach the situation in your own way. You may want all items of one category kept together: all dress coats, hats, and boots in the entry closet and all work coats, hats, and boots in the back hall. Or you may prefer to group items by users: all adult outerwear in the entry closet and children's things in the back hall or in their rooms.

Some people find it sensible to store spices in alphabetical order; some do the same with books and music. Determine a way to organize items that will make you comfortable. No one method is best; what's important is that your method work for you.

Devising a way to improve your storage situation gives you a framework to fall back on when you look at an object and wonder where to put it. If at some point your method seems less effective than it used to be, it's time to take a different approach.

KNOW WHAT YOU NEED: Although interest and activities change over time, people often forget to change their living spaces to match their lives. Often a storage problem develops because you've outgrown an interest but haven't gotten rid of its related equipment. Most families' basements, attics, and garages are repositories of outgrown skis, old tennis rackets, and out-of-date clothing.

A built-in sewing area is no longer useful if other interests have replaced sewing. A formal living room is wasted space if entertaining takes place in the family room.

The first step toward solving your storage problems is reviewing the pattern of your daily life to see what changes have occurred. Ultimately, improved storage frees you from dealing with too much stuff so you have time for more enjoyable activities.

One cardinal rule of developing storage is to put items near areas where you will use them. This small kitchen corner frames a writing desk, with drawers below for storing family records; open spaces above for mail, memos, and cookbooks; and cabinet space for rarely used dishes.

QUESTIONS TO ASK YOURSELF

What's the most frustrating area of your house? Where does the clutter accumulate? Your answers to these and the following questions will help you set priorities as you begin to get storage under control.

Do you have storage space for ongoing projects or hobbies, such as sewing, homework, quilting, painting, or woodworking? Do you have a safe place for mail, bills, recipes, and other household office items? Do such places have to be private or public?

Where do you put seasonal items—clothes, sports and hobby equipment, and lawn and garden items? Do you have a place for items in transit—recyclables, hand-me-downs, items for charity?

As you consider the things you store, run through this list:
■ Does it have to be accessible readily? Occasionally? Rarely?
■ Which family member uses the item most often?
■ Has anyone used it in the last 12 months? Will it be used again?

PLANNING EFFECTIVE SOLUTIONS

Start your planning process by searching for unused or underused spaces to add storage, as shown in the illustration below. Start with the obvious bare walls and corners, then search out unused nooks, insets, gaps, "next-to" areas (next to the door, next to the stove, etc.), and places above or below fixtures or appliances. Find areas that you can fill in and fit out without sacrificing floor space. No space is out of bounds; for example, you may be able to build storage in the space between studs of interior walls.

Examine all surfaces. The back of a door can be outfitted with a pocket organizer. The inside of a basement, attic, or laundry-room door can hold hooks and racks or be covered with perforated hardboard and hanging hooks.

Space under a staircase is ideal for storing bulky items. A coffee table (or any table at which no one sits) can hide games or magazines if the storage space can be masked from view.

Analyze your list of "must haves." Not everyone needs a dresser, for example. Maybe some shelves, baskets, and pocket organizers in a closet would clear out that dresser space. Do you need a permanent bed in the guest room, or could you use a sofa bed that takes up less space? This could create additional seating and free the room for other purposes.

Making an area serve more than one purpose increases your functional space. Can the recipe center in the kitchen become an all-purpose desk for homework? Can your sewing center, home office, or hobby area be a mobile cart on wheels?

Think also about the structure of your house and your household's needs. Would you

A careful inventory of the available space in your home can help you plan how to use it effectively. Compromises will be required.

prefer an open floor plan or specialized, private areas that are set apart?

CREATING ACCESS

Once you've decided on a potential storage space, determine its accessibility. Is it suitable for everyday items that require immediate access, or is it more appropriate for long-term storage? For example, if retrieving something from the attic involves setting up a stepladder and climbing through a trap door, the attic should be limited to storing rarely used items.

Easy access to items begins with storing them close to their point of use. Drinking glasses are difficult to carry, so why not store them directly above the dishwasher? Pots and pans should be kept close to the stove. Brooms, mops, and vacuum cleaners should be near the areas where they are used the most. Linens are best stored near the bedrooms and bathrooms. And magazines belong wherever your family enjoys reading.

A second level of access to items is how they are stowed within a storage area. Board games stacked 16 high at the back of a coat closet are not reached easily. Storage shelves should be convenient heights. For example, children should be able to reach their toys. Safe, secure locations should be found for dangerous items such as medicines, firearms, and chemicals.

TRAFFIC PATTERNS

The more you know about how you use your rooms, the better you can make them work for you. Take note of fixed elements in each room—the door openings, windows, closets, built-in cabinets, and other fixtures. They define the room's natural traffic patterns.

If you are considering a major reconfiguration of a room, start by making a floor plan of the space drawn to scale. Place tracing paper over the sketch and trace the walls and all the fixed elements mentioned above. Draw in the major traffic pathways between entry and exit doors, for example. Sketch the traffic patterns as if there were no furniture in the room. With a lighter pencil, draw secondary traffic routes, such as those that approach built-in features. These paths shape the room's activity areas. You may discover that these pathways cause just as many storage problems as crowding does.

Be sure you have easy access to items. In this case, it's not a good idea to store skis or ice skates hidden behind those summer sports items you just brought in for the winter. Make sure items are stored at a convenient height, too.

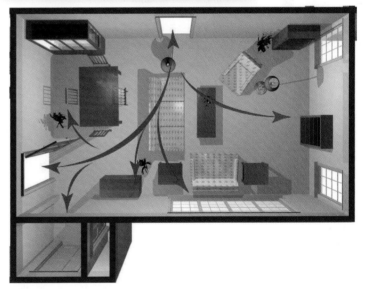

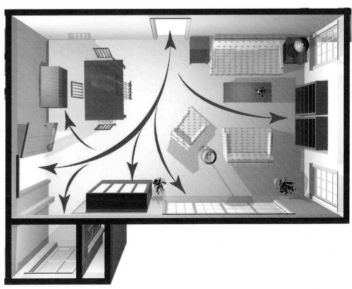

Analyze the traffic flow and furniture placement in a room before locating storage areas. If a storage space is hard to reach, it won't be used. The end result: more clutter.

PLANNING EFFECTIVE SOLUTIONS
continued

*On these floor-to-ceiling bookcases, **above**, you'd want to store children's books on the lower shelves and rarely-used books on the higher ones.*

***RIGHT:** The informal country style of this kitchen has the added benefit of keeping dishes and other tableware right at hand.*

CONSIDER DIMENSIONS

Once you have clear access to a storage area, the next challenge is to make it easy to retrieve things and put them back. This is where the height and depth of shelves, counters, and closet rods come in.

Although occupants of a home come in different sizes and shapes, most homes are built for the average-size person. Standard kitchen counters are 36 inches high. Yet the people who use them might be much more comfortable if the counters were lower, say 32 inches, or higher, about 40 inches. By the same token, if a closet rod is too high for a child to reach, clothes probably won't get hung up. Objects crammed into spaces that are too small will not only be difficult to reach but may suffer damage. The ideal dimensions for any storage unit are those that suit the people who use it and the objects it will hold.

FORM AND FUNCTION

Another consideration in planning your storage space is style. What do you want to display or hide? Do you prefer formal or informal arrangements? Your goal should be to harmonize your storage spaces with the architectural and furnishing style of your home. Fortunately, you have a lot of flexibility in this area. For example, the warm, informal American country style incorporates open storage for dinnerware, pans, crockery, and foodstuffs. A purely utilitarian, industrial style also emphasizes display. Both are "bones-out" styles. On the other hand, traditional wood kitchen cabinets may provide completely covered storage—even the refrigerator door might be covered with a matching wood veneer. A contemporary all-laminate kitchen may accomplish the same thing. Both strongly emphasize a finished look.

Every style provides options for displaying or concealing stored items. Formal styles may set the stage for elegant display, and informal styles may emphasize the lived-in look. Both allow you to choose what to reveal and what to conceal.

*Your personal style plays a large role in planning storage solutions. This industrial-style kitchen has the same "bones-out" functional focus as the country-style **above**, but its character is much different.*

STORAGE FROM STORES

Throughout this book are many projects you can build to enhance your storage. But before you build, you may want to investigate sources of prebuilt or ready-to-build storage solutions.

Most home centers, lumberyards, and discount stores stock shelving material and hardware; ready-to-assemble shelves, bookcases, computer desks, and entertainment centers; and many other storage systems. Among the most popular of these kit storage solutions are modular closet organization systems, made of either plastic-coated metal grids or wood.

Another source of items—and ideas—are catalogue businesses and stores that specialize in storage products. These businesses stock many ready-made and kit storage solutions. They also have consultants who will help you plan solutions based on the products they stock or can order from various distributors. Browsing through these shops and catalogues can provide you with many ideas.

Antique dealers and used furniture stores are another source of storage solutions. Even if you're not an antique collector, you may find a solution to one of your problems.

Before you build, explore the storage units now available at home centers, discount stores, and specialty storage stores.

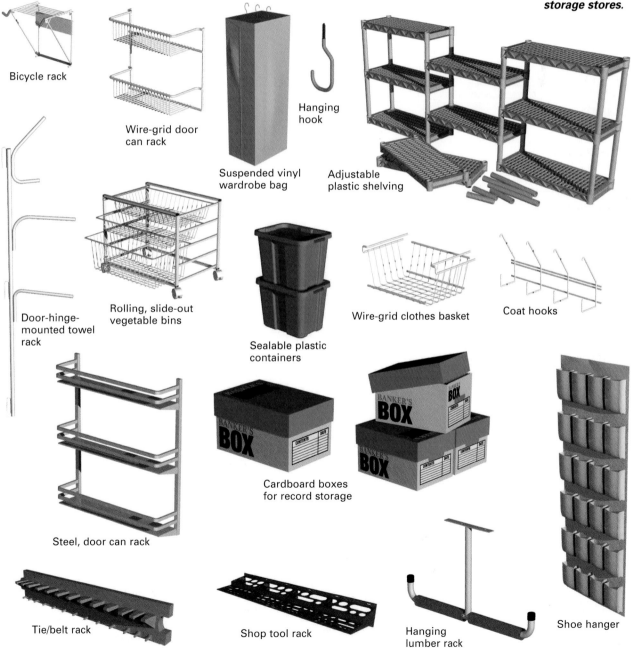

Bicycle rack

Wire-grid door can rack

Suspended vinyl wardrobe bag

Hanging hook

Adjustable plastic shelving

Door-hinge-mounted towel rack

Rolling, slide-out vegetable bins

Sealable plastic containers

Wire-grid clothes basket

Coat hooks

Steel, door can rack

Cardboard boxes for record storage

Shoe hanger

Tie/belt rack

Shop tool rack

Hanging lumber rack

BASIC TECHNIQUES

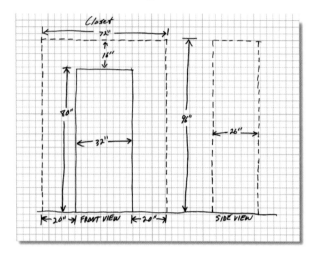

SIZING UP YOUR SPACES

Once you've decided where to add storage, your next step is to size up the space. Using graph paper, draw the room or a portion of it and sketch in the major features, such as walls, doorways, windows, and other fixed items. Measure and record the height, width, and depth of these features. Add detailed items, such as trim, if necessary. The best tool for this job is a 1-inch wide, 16- or 25-foot steel tape measure. The more you know about the space, the better off you'll be when you draw your detailed plans. You can then use the sketch of the space as the base for a detailed drawing of your project.

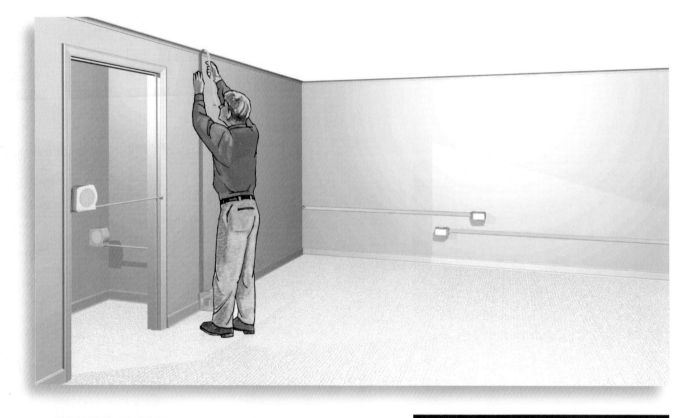

PLUMB, FLAT, AND LEVEL

Before you draw detailed plans of your project, you need to determine if walls, floors, and openings are plumb (truly vertical), level (truly horizontal), square (perpendicular to one another), and parallel to one another. If not, you'll need to compensate for these differences in your plan or correct the problems before you begin building the project. A 2- or 4-foot carpenter's level and a framing square are essential tools for this job.

MATERIALS FOR STORAGE PROJECTS

For most of the projects you may tackle, you'll be using one of two types of basic wood materials: lumber or sheet goods.

LUMBER: Lumber is classified as either boards—less than 2 inches thick and wider than 3 inches—or dimension lumber—more than 2 inches thick and wide. You can choose a softwood, such as pine or fir, which is easy to work with. Hardwoods, such as birch, oak, or cherry, have more character but are harder to work with.

Lumber has both nominal and actual dimensions. For example, a 2×4 is actually $1\frac{1}{2}\times3\frac{1}{2}$ inches and a 1×6 is $\frac{3}{4}\times5\frac{1}{2}$ inches. Order by nominal size, but design your project with actual size in mind.

SHEET GOODS: Sheet goods include plywood, particleboard or waferboard, hardboard, or laminate-covered panels.

■ PLYWOOD is made of layers (plies) of wood glued together with their grains running in alternate directions, which makes the finished product strong. Plywood is sold in 4x8-foot sheets in thicknesses ranging from $\frac{1}{8}$ inch up to $1\frac{1}{8}$ inches. For shelves and other projects in this book, the most common thicknesses required will be $\frac{1}{4}$-, $\frac{1}{2}$-, and $\frac{3}{4}$-inch material.

Plywood is graded on both its surfaces: "A" being the smoothest and free of defects and "B," "C," and "D" are progressively rougher. Both sides need not be graded the same (for example, A-C). You'll want an "A" surface for the finished side of most projects.

■ PARTICLEBOARD AND HARDBOARD are made of wood chips, fibers, and glue bonded together under heat and pressure. They are sold in 4×8-foot sheets in thicknesses from $\frac{1}{8}$ inch up to $\frac{3}{4}$ inch. They are less expensive than plywood but often harder to work with because screws and nails do not hold well in their edges, which have no continuous grain. Particle board can be used for shelving, cabinets, and as core material for countertops. You can also buy particle board or plywood that is covered with plastic laminate, eliminating the need to finish the surface.

■ DRYWALL, often called wallboard, is used to finish walls. You'll need it to make repairs if you cut into a wall for a project.

GLASS: An alternative material for shelves is decorative glass. Do not use regular window pane glass; buy plate glass designed to be used for tabletops and shelves.

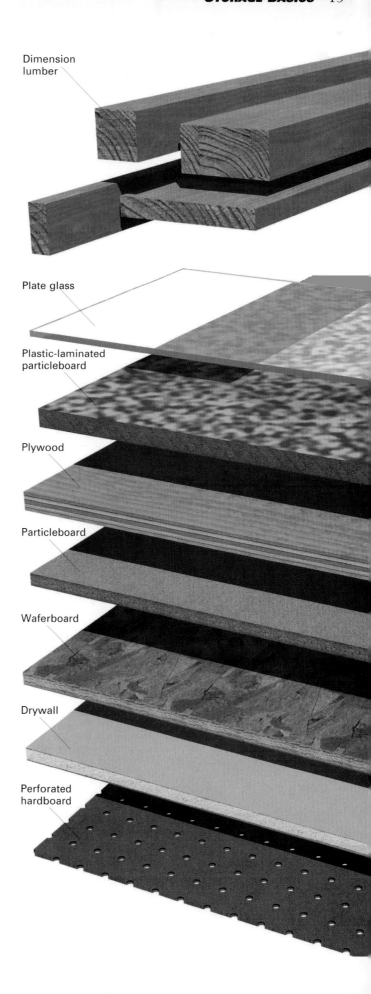

Dimension lumber

Plate glass

Plastic-laminated particleboard

Plywood

Particleboard

Waferboard

Drywall

Perforated hardboard

MATERIALS FOR DO-IT-YOURSELF STORAGE PROJECTS
continued

BASIC TOOLS FOR BUILDING YOUR STORAGE SOLUTIONS

To build the projects in this book or to tackle your own storage solutions, you should assemble a basic tool kit. Complement this kit with other tools as you need them.

For measuring and marking, you should include a 16- or 25-foot, 1-inch-wide tape measure; a plumb bob; a chalk line; and a pencil.

To make sure things stay plumb, level, and square, you'll need a 2- or 4-foot carpenter's level, a framing square, and a combination or speed square to help mark cuts.

For cutting materials, a crosscut handsaw will do, but you'll probably want to invest in a 12- or 13-amp, 7¼-inch circular saw. A backsaw and miter box are essential if you'll be cutting a lot of miter joints. A keyhole saw is the best hand tool for cutting holes in drywall, and a coping saw or variable-speed jigsaw is a useful power tool for cutting curves and designs.

For fastening, invest in 16-ounce claw hammer for nailing. Have a nail set on hand for driving nailheads below the surface of finished work. Have a good assortment of screwdrivers, including No. 1 and No. 2 Phillips heads and at least two sizes of slot-tipped ones. Make pilot holes for screws with an awl.

You'll need a power drill to bore holes. Buy a variable-speed drill with a ⅜-inch chuck. Drill bits to have on hand include twist bits for pilot holes, spade bits for general purpose drilling, and a combination wood drill countersink. You may also want brad-point bits for doweling and shelf holes and a plug cutter to cut plugs to cover countersunk screw heads. Buy Phillips-, slot-, and square-head screwdriver bits for your drill and you can drive screws faster and more easily than by hand.

A router is a very versatile power tool. Use it to cut dadoes, mortises, and dovetails for strong shelf joints. It's also the best tool to trim laminate edges on shelves and countertops.

You'll need an assortment of clamps—C-clamps, squeeze clamps, and adjustable clamps—to hold glued items together while they set.

For shaping and finishing, your tool kit should include a wood file and rasp, chisels, block plane, and hand-sanding block. A power orbital or belt sander also is a good investment if you're finishing large surfaces.

FASTENERS, HARDWARE, AND STORAGE COMPONENTS

Fastening materials, hardware, and other components for building storage solutions vary considerably with the type and extent of your project.

Basic fasteners include, of course, nails and screws. For general construction, use box or common nails. For finish work, use finish nails or brads, sinking their heads below the surface with a nail set.

Wood screws are made with flat, oval, or round heads. Use ovalhead or roundhead screws with trim washers when the head will be exposed to view. Use flathead screws when they will be countersunk. Screwhead types include slotted, Phillips, or square-drive styles. Phillips are perhaps the easiest to drive and can be driven with an electric drill. You may need lag screws, hanger screws, machine bolts, toggle bolts, hollow-wall anchors, or masonry anchors to fasten projects to walls.

You can strengthen joints with angle brackets, flat corner irons, T-plates, or mending plates. Corrugated fasteners, wooden dowels, or biscuits also can be used to strengthen miter, butt, or dado joints.

The variety of shelf-bracket systems ranges from basic closet-rod brackets to several styles of slotted, adjustable standards and accompanying interlocking shelf brackets. You also can support shelves by simply drilling parallel sets of holes and inserting one of many types of pin supports.

If you're building a cabinet, you may need to select hinges and catches for the doors, slides the for drawers, and pulls and knobs for both.

SHELF-HANGING HARDWARE

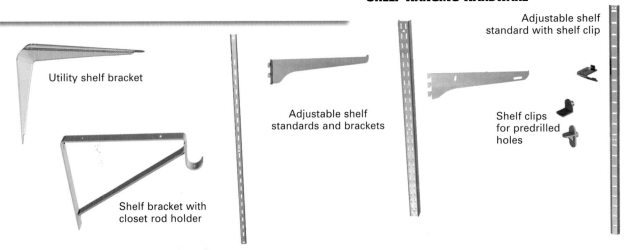

Utility shelf bracket

Shelf bracket with closet rod holder

Adjustable shelf standards and brackets

Adjustable shelf standard with shelf clip

Shelf clips for predrilled holes

FASTENERS

Box nail

Carriage bolt

Common nail

Corrugated fastener

Masonry lag shield

Drywall screw

Plastic wall anchor

Finish nail

Toggle bolt

Trim washer

Brad

Hanger screw

Lag screw

Machine bolt

Roundhead screw

Washer

Phillips head screw

Slot head screw

CABINETRY HARDWARE

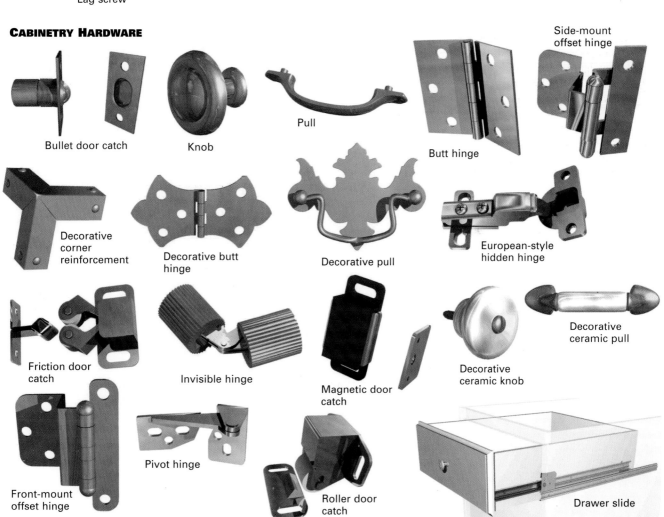

Bullet door catch

Knob

Pull

Butt hinge

Side-mount offset hinge

Decorative corner reinforcement

Decorative butt hinge

Decorative pull

European-style hidden hinge

Friction door catch

Invisible hinge

Magnetic door catch

Decorative ceramic knob

Decorative ceramic pull

Front-mount offset hinge

Pivot hinge

Roller door catch

Drawer slide

BUILDING BASIC UNITS

INSTALLING SHELVES

Once you've made your general plan, it's time to create specific storage units. Shelving, the most common storage solution, uses vertical space to store items so they are out of the way yet accessible.

Before you buy lumber and build your own shelving, take some time to investigate the wide selection of ready-made shelving available at home centers. You'll find precut shelves in various lengths made from softwood, hardwood, particle board, and laminated particle board. All these choices are quick and simple to install and are prefinished so you don't have to worry about sanding and painting or staining the final product. Most shelves are manufactured to fit common-size shelf brackets and wall standards.

In planning shelving, consult the table below to calculate the spans, which are based on the load you expect the shelf to bear. If you're selecting ready-made shelves, be sure they'll handle the load or make sure to use additional supports to reduce the spans.

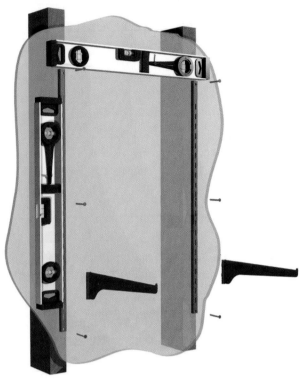

Use a magnetic or electronic stud sensor to locate the wall's framing lumber, which will support your shelf system. At one stud, mark the top of one standard. Drive the top screw of the standard into the stud. Using a level to determine plumb, secure the bottom of the standard. Place the level on top of the standard and mark the locations of the tops of the other standards. Install the remaining standards, then insert the brackets. If a standard must be mounted where there is no stud, your hardware dealer can provide an appropriate wall anchor.

SHELF LOADS AND SPANS

A shelf's potential for sagging depends on how much load it will bear. A shelf full of books requires more supports (shorter spans) or thicker shelving material than a shelf holding linens. The span length also depends on whether the load is concentrated in the center of the shelf or distributed along the length of the span.

Material		Maximum Span With Heavy Load	Maximum Span With Light Load
³⁄₈-inch plate glass	6 inches wide	15 inches	24 inches
	12 inches wide	18 inches	36 inches
¹⁄₂-inch acrylic plastic	6 inches wide	18 inches	30 inches
	12 inches wide	20 inches	36 inches
1-inch lumber	6 inches wide	18 inches	36 inches
	12 inches wide	24 inches	48 inches
³⁄₄-inch particle board	6 inches wide	20 inches	36 inches
	12 inches wide	28 inches	48 inches
³⁄₄-inch plywood	6 inches wide	24 inches	48 inches
	12 inches wide	36 inches	54 inches
2-inch lumber	6 inches wide	36 inches	48 inches
	12 inches wide	48 inches	60 inches

THE BOX

The next step beyond a basic shelf is a box. Whether it's a storage cube, the outside frame of a bookcase, a toy or hope chest, or a drawer in a cabinet, its basic form is a box.

The keys to building a good box are strong corner joints and making sure the box is square. A butt joint is the simplest way to form a corner: The face of one board is joined to the edge of another. For the more attractive rabbet joint, one board is recessed into a groove cut into another board. In a miter joint, the most attractive but also the weakest joint, the edge of each corner board is cut at a 45-degree angle.

To make joints stronger, you can reinforce them with angle brackets, flat corner irons, wooden cleats, corrugated fasteners, or wooden dowels or biscuits. Miter joints are especially weak and should be reinforced with one of these methods.

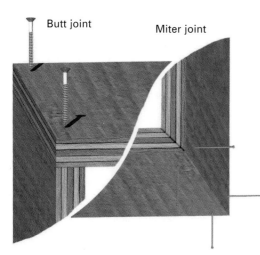

Butt joint

Miter joint

Select the style of joint you will use and cut your materials to size. Place one side in position against the top piece and predrill holes for screws or nails. You may want to countersink the holes if you are using screws. Screw the pieces together and repeat the process on the other side and top piece. You can use carpenter's glue to increase the strength of the joint.

Before the glue dries on the joints, test the box corners with a framing square. Double check by measuring from one corner to the opposite corner. Then measure the distance for the other diagonal. If the measurements are not equal, the box is not square.

*Once the corners are square, place adjustable clamps across the sides and from top to bottom and let the glue dry. After the joints have dried, you can add reinforcing brackets as shown, **above left**.*

BUILDING BASIC UNITS

continued

This freestanding bookcase is remarkably simple. However, the construction is complex enough to offer a challenge— an opportunity to master a number of woodworking techniques.

When determining the size of a bookcase, consider the lines and proportions of the room in which it will be located. A bookcase that is the same height as a door or that aligns with the tops of windows, for example, will harmonize with the room. The freestanding bookcase described here is 30 inches wide and 60 inches high, but you can alter the size to fit your needs.

Shelves longer than 30 inches may sag unless they are reinforced. For a bookcase wider than 30 inches, add shelf supports along the back of each shelf. An option is to build two bookcases and stand them side by side to create an illusion of a single, large unit.

This bookcase is made of ¾-inch cabinet-grade (A-A) oak plywood. You may prefer to construct the case from 1× or ⁵⁄₄ solid lumber. The case has a face frame to make it more rigid and to cover the exposed edges of the plywood. The face frame, however, is not a structural element.

PREPARING THE PIECES: Rip three boards, 11 inches wide, from a sheet of the oak plywood. From these, cut two side pieces, each 60 inches long, and the top and bottom shelves, each 29¼ inches long. Rip plywood shelves 10½ inches wide. The shelves are narrower than the other pieces to allow for the ¼-inch-thick back and the ¼-inch shelf trim that hides the front edges of the plywood.

Lay the two side pieces, back edges together, with the inside surfaces facing up. Measure and mark the positions of the top

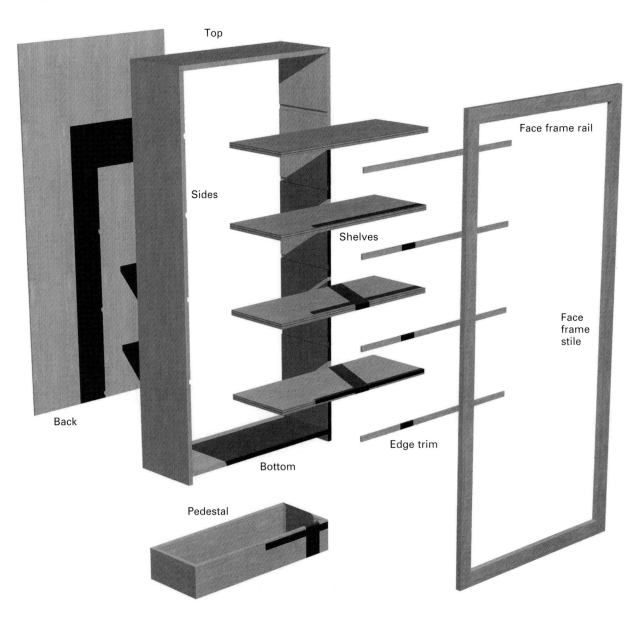

Top

Face frame rail

Sides

Shelves

Face frame stile

Back

Edge trim

Bottom

Pedestal

piece, allowing for a ⅜-inch rabbet and the bottom shelf, 1½ inches from the bottom edge. Carefully join the marks across the full width of both boards.

These lines must be square and true and the side pieces must match exactly.

Mark the positions of all four shelves in the same way. In this case, the shelves are 15, 27, 39, and 50 inches from the bottom, but you can change the shelf heights as you prefer.

In each side piece, cut ¾-inch-wide by ⅜-inch-deep grooves or tracks, called *dadoes*, in which to insert the shelves. Then cut ⅜-inch rabbets for the top piece. Cut a ⅜-inch-wide and ¼-inch-deep notch, or *rabbet*, along the back edge of the top, side, and bottom pieces to accommodate the back panel. If you prefer adjustable shelves (*see "Making Your Shelves Adjustable" on page 20*), rabbet and dado only the top of the case and the bottom shelf. Cut the intermediate shelves to 28¼ inches to allow for maneuvering them in and out of the case. Sand and prepare all the surfaces before continuing the assembly.

TRIM THE SHELVES: To trim the shelves, cut four ¼×¾-inch strips from 1×2 solid oak. Cut each strip the length of each shelf. Apply glue to the front edges of the shelves and the back edges of the strips. Attach the strips to the shelves with 3d finish nails. Set the nail heads, then fill the holes with wood putty. Remove excess glue. When dry, sand the trim flush with the shelf surface.

An alternative trim is oak veneer tape, which you iron onto the edges of the shelves. In this case, you would have to cut the shelf a bit wider.

ASSEMBLE THE CASE: Spread glue on one end of the top piece and in the top rabbet of one side piece. Set the top piece in the rabbet, making sure the rabbets in the back edge face forward. Nail together with 6d finish nails: three nails into the sides and two through the top.

Spread glue on the dado for the bottom shelf. Set the shelf in place, making sure the rabbet on the back is facing up, and nail from the outside with 6d nails. Attach the interior shelves as you did the bottom shelf. To attach the other side piece, spread glue in the dadoes and rabbets and fit the top piece and shelves into place, nailing as you did on the first side.

For the back panel, cut a sheet of ¼-inch plywood to 29¼×59¼ inches. Sand the front side of the panel. With the bookcase resting on its front edges, glue and nail the back panel into place.

Clamp the case, remove all excess glue, and let it dry.

MATERIALS LIST

Item	Material	Dimensions	Qty
Sides	¾" A-A plywood	11×60"	2
Top, bottom	¾" A-A plywood	11×29¼"	2
Shelves	¾" A-A plywood	10½ ×29¼"	4
Edge trim	¼×¾" solid oak	29¼"	4
Back	¼" A-C plywood	29¼×59¼"	1
Face stiles	1×2" solid oak	60"	2
Face rails	1×2" solid oak	27"	2
Face fasteners	¼" dowels	2"	8
Pedestal sides	¾" A-A plywood	5×10¾"	2
Pedestal front, back	¾" A-A plywood	5×28½"	2

3d, 4d, and 6d smooth finish nails; 1½" #6 drywall screws; 3" #8 drywall screws; white glue; wood putty; stain or paint

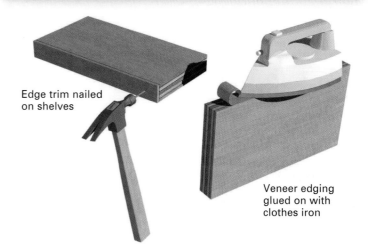

Edge trim nailed on shelves

Veneer edging glued on with clothes iron

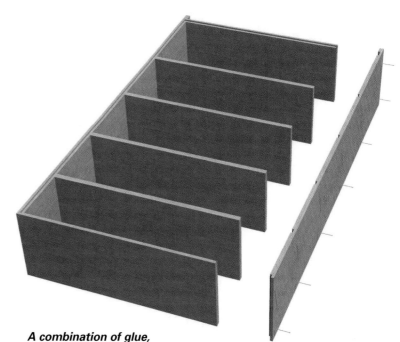

A combination of glue, dadoes, and nails ensures that these shelves will stay straight and square.

BUILDING BASIC UNITS
continued

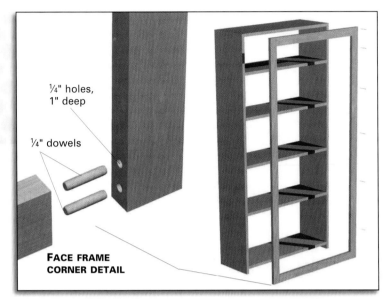

1/4" holes, 1" deep

1/4" dowels

**FACE FRAME
CORNER DETAIL**

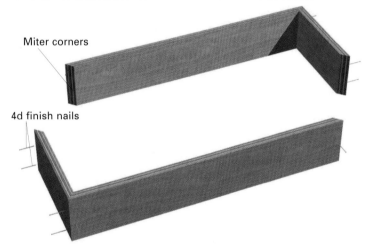

Miter corners

4d finish nails

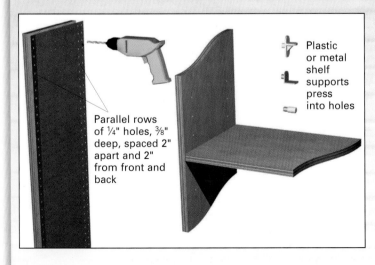

MAKE THE FACE FRAME: Cut the face frame pieces to length from 1×2 oak. The rails should fit exactly inside the stiles when the stiles are flush with the outside edges of the case. Measure carefully. On a flat surface, align the rails squarely inside the stiles.

Using a square, mark two lines across each joint. Using a doweling jig, drill 1/4-inch holes 1-inch deep at the marks. Apply glue to the rails along the end grain and in the dowel holes, tap in the dowels, and tap the assembly together. Check for square, clamp, remove excess glue, and let dry.

Apply glue to the front edges of the bookcase. Fit the face frame to the case so the outside edges are flush and the bottom rail aligns with the top of the lowest shelf. Nail the frame on the case with 6d finish nails. Set the nails and fill the holes. Remove excess glue and let dry.

MAKE THE PEDESTAL: From the leftover oak plywood, cut four 5-inch-wide pieces, two 28 1/2 inches long, and two 10 3/4 inches long. Miter each of the ends at 45 degrees. Spread glue on the miters on one short and one long piece. Fit them together and cross-nail them with 4d finish nails. Fasten the other two pieces in the same manner. Then fasten the two L-shaped pieces together. Remove excess glue, check for square, clamp, and let dry.

Position the pedestal under the bookcase so the face frame and sides overlap it equally. For added stability, screw 1 1/2-inch drywall screws through the bottom shelf into the pedestal.

MAKING YOUR SHELVES ADJUSTABLE

Plastic or metal shelf supports press into holes

Parallel rows of 1/4" holes, 3/8" deep, spaced 2" apart and 2" from front and back

If you'd prefer to have adjustable shelves in a bookcase or shelf unit, do not cut dadoes for the shelves. Drill a series of 1/4-inch holes in the sides of the case. The holes should be 3/8-inch deep, 2 inches apart vertically, and 2 inches from the front and back. You must be sure that the holes line up exactly in both rows and on both boards, or the shelves will not be level. An easy way to ensure this is to use a template made out of perforated hardboard. Lay the hardboard on the side pieces, using the holes as a drilling guide.

Then simply purchase one of the many styles of plastic or metal pin-type shelf supports on which to rest the shelves.

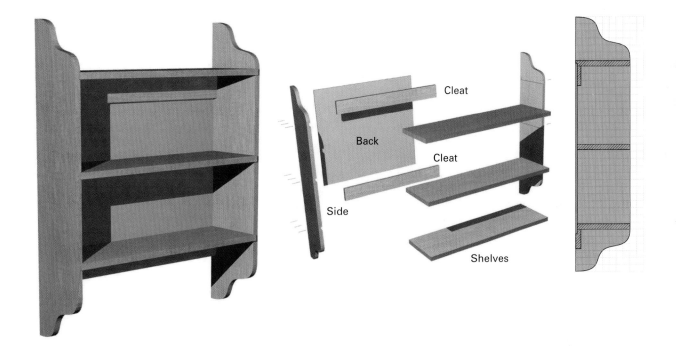

BUILDING A HANGING BOOKSHELF

A hanging bookshelf is an excellent way to display and store items in virtually any area of your home. You can store cookbooks and spices in the kitchen, books and collectibles in the family room, dishes in the dining room, and soaps, perfumes, and small bouquets in the bathroom.

The 36-inch-high, 28-inch-wide bookshelf shown here is designed to hang from two studs, either 16 inches or 24 inches apart. You can adapt the dimensions to your needs. Select No. 2 pine boards, without large knots or warping, so you can stain, oil, or paint the bookshelf to match other furniture.

Cut the uprights and shelves to length. Rip ¼ inch from the center shelf to allow for the recessed plywood back. Cut the back out of ¼-inch A-C plywood to 27¼ inches wide by

24¼ inches high—¾ inch less than the total width of the cabinet and ¾ inch shorter than the distance between the top of the top shelf and the bottom of the bottom shelf. Use 1×3s for cleats.

Use a jigsaw to cut the ornamental curves at the ends of the side pieces. File and sand the curves to remove any saw marks.

Position the uprights so their back edges meet and the inside surfaces are facing up. Mark the top and bottom of each shelf dado. Set a ¾-inch dado blade or a ¾-inch router bit to a depth of ¼ inch and cut the dadoes. Saw or rout a ⅜-inch-wide × ¼-inch-deep rabbet on the back edges of the uprights for the plywood back to sit in.

Assemble the shelves by applying glue to the ends of the shelves and the dadoes. Insert the shelves, then drive in 6d finish nails through the uprights into each shelf. Set the nails below the surface, then cover the holes with wood putty.

Cut the cleats to match the inside width of the case. Apply glue to the upper edges and ends, then secure the cleats to the case with 4d finish nails through the sides and through the shelves. Rout a ¼-inch rabbet into the back of the top and bottom shelves. Spread glue along the rabbets and on the back face of each cleat. Then screw or nail the back to the case. Now you can sand and paint.

To hang the bookshelf, drill countersunk holes through the cleats where you intend to drive screws into the wall studs. Drive in 3-inch drywall screws through each of the cleats into the studs. Fill the holes with putty or insert a wood plug to cover the screwheads.

MATERIALS LIST

Item	Material	Dimensions	Qty
Sides	1×8 pine	36"	2
Shelves	1×8 pine	27"	2
Cleats	1×3 pine	26½"	4
Back	¼" A-C ply	24¼×27¼"	1

4d smooth finish nails; 3" #8 drywall screws; white carpenter's glue; wood putty; stain or paint

BUILDING BASIC UNITS
continued

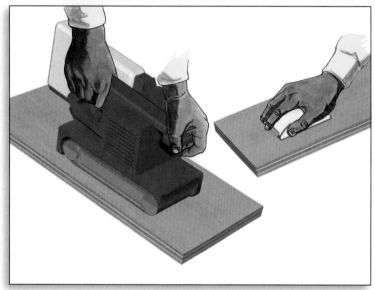

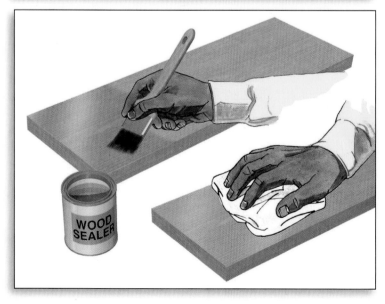

The key to achieving an ideal finish is careful preparation of the surface. Stains, clear finishes, and even paint won't cover up imperfections in the wood. So don't skip quickly over these details.

On bookcases, cabinets, or other storage projects that have fixed shelves or tight corners, you may want to undertake these surface-finishing steps before assembly.

FILLING AND SMOOTHING: The first step is to fill small scratches and gaps and nail holes. If you are going to paint the piece, use acetone-based wood putty or latex paste wood filler. Apply these with a flat putty knife, pushing the filler into the gap or hole, then scraping away the excess. The goal is a smooth surface—no lumps should show under the primer and paint. An oil-based crayon makes quick work of filling small holes.

If you use a clear finish or stain rather than paint, select the filler carefully. Patched areas will take a stain or finish differently than the surrounding solid wood. It's best to test fillers, stains, and the finish coat on a scrap of your project's wood to find the best match.

SANDING: Repairing, sanding, and cleaning wood surfaces are tedious tasks, but they are important to any project, so take your time. Begin sanding with a rough (80-grit) abrasive paper and move to 120- or 180-grit. Seal the wood again, then sand again with extra-fine paper (220- or 400-grit) for the smoothest surface. Electric sanders save time but tend to leave marks or grooves, so plan to do the final sanding by hand. Remember to sand with, not against, the wood's natural grain

SEALING AND STAINING: A sealer helps close the wood's pores, which results in an even stain or paint finish. It also serves as an intermediate coat between the stain and the final finish. This is especially important for stains that react with and ooze into the finish. A sealer is sufficient protection on articles made of particleboard for use in a basement or garage. Apply sealer with a brush, working it into the grain in all directions.

Stains add color and enhance the natural grain of the wood. Except for penetrating oil stains, a stain doesn't protect the wood so you'll want to use a top coat of shellac, varnish, or oil for that purpose. Stains can be applied with a brush or cloth. After your piece stands for a while, wipe off the excess.

THE RIGHT FINISH

The final finish on your project gives smoothness, sheen (high, medium, or low), and sometimes color, as well as protection for the piece. Natural-resin or polyurethane varnishes, shellac, lacquer, wax, oils, stains, and gloss or enamel paints are among the options. When selecting a finishing product, consider all the factors, including the type of project; its style, use, and location; and the look you desire.

FINISHES FOR THE PROJECT

Material	Description	Use	Application	Comments
Paint, gloss or enamel finish	Opaque, usually oil- or synthetic based, liquid that dries to a hard finish	Colors and protects wood	Brush, spray	Wood must be sealed or primed; apply two or more coats; sand with abrasive paper or steel wool between coats
Varnish, natural-resin or polyurethane	Clear Finish; new synthetic (polyurethane) varnishes superior to traditional formulations	Enhances appearance of and protects wood	Varnish brush for natural-resin types; brush, spray polyurethanes	Durable finish; shows off depth and grain pattern of wood; resists moisture, including alcoholic beverages; fairly slow drying
Shellac	Clear to slightly cloudy finish	Protects raw or stained wood; used as a sanding sealer or sealer under stain or paint	Brush, spray	Similar to varnish in protective and visual qualities, but dries faster; clean up with ammonia and warm water or alcohol
Lacquer	Clear protective finish	Workable finish for fine furniture	Spray; apply three coats, rubbing with steel wool between coats; leave final coat glossy or rub to a satin finish	Use wood filler to create smooth base first; extremely fast drying time simplifies application of multiple coats
Water-based stain	Powder or premixed liquid; well suited to enhancing grain of premium hardwoods	Tints wood	Brush, spread with cloth, spray; dampen wood first	Designed to be used under protective clear finish
Pigmented oil stain	Premixed liquid	Tints wood	Brush or wipe on; wipe off excess	Well suited for darker tints on softwoods; when dry, apply clear finish for protection
Alcohol or spirit stain	Powder or premixed liquid	Mostly commercial; use fine spray for shading	Spray	Use in spray applicator for shading and refinishing
Penetrating oil stain	Linseed or tung oil-based premixed liquid	Tints and protects wood	Brush, cloth	Apply paste was for added luster and protection
Wax	Paste compound that dries to hard, lustrous finish	Protects oiled finishes	Cloth, buff with clean cloth	Wax finish over a penetrating oil stain gives warm, lustrous appearance
Oil	Linseed, tung or plastic based; produces translucent to dark tints	Colors wood and gives it harder surface	Brush on; wipe off with cloth	Soaks into wood and gives warm, lustrous appearance

Roll-up cabinets in this modern kitchen put storage where you need it, right in front of the cook. Rarely-used items are stored in high cupboards. Plenty of low-level cabinets meet storage needs for often-used items.

BELOW: *This sewing, ironing, and laundry center includes a space for everything. If you don't have the luxury of a separate room for such purposes, this chapter offers some options.*

KITCHENS, BATHROOMS, LAUNDRY AND UTILITY ROOMS

IN THIS SECTION

The Kitchen **26**
Bathrooms **36**
Laundry and Utility
Rooms **40**

In most homes, kitchens and bathrooms get the most use, and laundry and utility rooms gather the most clutter. All four spaces cry out for storage solutions.

A hard-working kitchen requires space for fresh and canned foods, spices, utensils, flatware, napkins, tableware, and serving dishes. Then there's that arsenal of appliances, which seems to grow in the wake of infomercials and holidays. Carving out a place for these items can enhance your storage capacity and make cooking more enjoyable.

Bathrooms have their own storage challenges. Squeezing towels and linens, hair curlers and dryers, and a drugstore of health care items into limited space stretches anyone's creativity—and tolerance.

Laundry and utility areas—whether in various rooms or relegated to one—tend to fill up as quickly as a backyard pool fills up with neighbors. If you don't have a storage plan for these rooms, things can get out of hand. Fortunately, you can build or buy storage units that restore order to your home.

Take advantage of nooks and crannies in bathrooms and hallways. With careful planning and a little do-it-yourself carpentry, it's amazing how much you can store in a small space.

THE KITCHEN

Most kitchens rely on cabinets for storage space. The challenge is to organize that space to increase its peak efficiency.

Kitchens generally are organized around three work centers: food preparation, cooking, and cleanup. Kitchen designers plan efficient kitchens by trying to achieve a balanced work triangle—a comfortable distance—between these three centers.

If you're buying cabinets, look into the specialty items available: lazy susans and lift-out shelves for appliances, below; drawers for canned goods that take advantage of narrow spaces, opposite.

STORE ITEMS WHERE THEY ARE USED

The first step toward improving the efficiency of kitchen storage is to store items close to the work center where you will use them.

Cabinets near the food preparation area should contain such staples as flour and sugar, spices, and other baking supplies; mixing utensils, bowls, and measuring spoons and cups; and baking tins, cookie sheets, and casserole dishes. Here you'll also want room for your food preparation appliances: mixers, food processors, and blenders.

Pots, pans, and other cookware; specialty cooking appliances such as griddles, crockpots, or fryers; and serving dishes should be stored near the range or oven.

The sink and dishwasher mark the center of the cleanup area. Near them you should have cleaning supplies, the wastebasket or trash compactor, and kitchen linens. It's also good to locate flatware, dishes, and glasses

near the dishwasher so you don't have to cart them across the kitchen to put them away.

BOOSTING CABINET CAPACITY

Standard base and wall cabinets hold great untapped potential for storage. Most 30- to 36-inch cabinets have double doors and one or two interior shelves. There are many ways to use this space more efficiently. You can buy or build deep pullout organizers, vertical dividers for trays, shallow drawers for utensils, lazy susans of all sizes, and racks and half-moon trays that fit on the insides of cabinet doors. Decide what you need to store in a given cabinet, then plan accordingly. You'll be surprised how much more you can store in what has been wasted space.

KITCHEN SPECIALTY PRODUCTS

Storage solutions don't all rely on adding space; the most innovative ideas involve using space that might normally be wasted. This ovenside drawer is extra useful because it is so convenient.

When you start to organize your kitchen cabinets, study the products in specialty storage stores and major home centers. Freestanding islands, such as the one above, can be built or purchased. In many cases, they can be covered with a surface that matches your kitchen countertops. And this type of island can be moved to suit your changing needs.

THE KITCHEN
continued

Kitchen shelves don't have to be enclosed. This country-style cabinet provides storage and display space. Its placement right above the sink makes putting away dishes an easy task.

Pantry cabinets come in many configurations—fixed shelves, multitiered lazy susans, door racks, or swing-out or pullout shelves. You also can retrofit existing ones.

INCREASING CABINET CAPACITY

Peninsula or island cabinets with access on more than one side are especially convenient in a kitchen with multiple cooks. A new peninsula or island can easily have this feature built in, or the units can be retrofitted with pullout trays that open both ways. Open shelving is a natural at the end of a peninsula or an island.

Everyday dishes and tableware need not be hidden behind closed doors. More efficient places to store such items include open shelves, small cubicles, or vertical plate racks near the dishwasher or dining area. Keeping often-used items within easy reach makes sense and adds a decorative touch. Changing dishes with the season gives you a built-in change in decor as well. Vertical plate racks and cup shelves at the right height are pleasing alternatives to blank cabinet doors.

PARK YOUR APPLIANCES

Portable appliances are like national defense systems: You don't want to see them constantly, but you want to know they're available for duty on a moment's notice. Each appliance needs a home of its own without intruding into other storage or work space. Parking appliances on the counter in a closed garage places them out of sight yet ready for use in an instant. You can use a straight

garage or make the most of a corner with a diagonal appliance garage. Garages can contain electrical outlets on the rear walls to keep cords out of sight. Door choices include hinged doors or roll-up tambour doors, which further cut down on clutter.

STORE SPICES IN RACKS

Although spices can be attractive when kept in full view, their strength and flavor are diminished by exposure to light. Consider a drawer insert or a slide-out vertical cabinet. A spice rack mounted inside a cabinet door keeps spices within easy reach, although the cabinet shelves probably will have to be altered to accommodate the rack. lazy susans offer convenient and accessible spice storage.

USE BINS OR METAL-LINED DRAWERS

Tip-out vegetable bins solve the need to store potatoes and onions in cool darkness. Metal-lined bins, now available from many cabinet companies, are modern versions of the pie safes, bread boxes, and flour bins of our grandparents' kitchens. Having often-used food items tucked away in a roll-out or tip-out drawer or bin makes them even more convenient and frees up both counter and cabinet space.

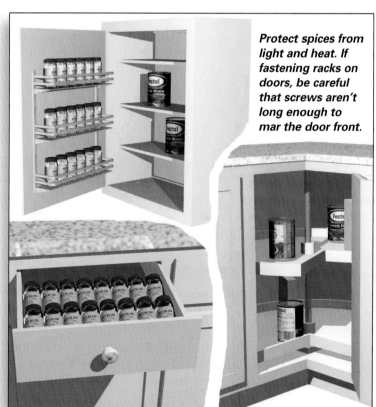

Protect spices from light and heat. If fastening racks on doors, be careful that screws aren't long enough to mar the door front.

Storage bays keep countertops clear and appliances dust-free.

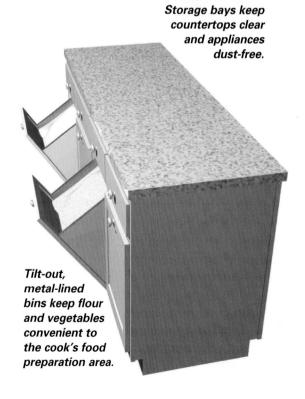

Tilt-out, metal-lined bins keep flour and vegetables convenient to the cook's food preparation area.

THE KITCHEN
continued

Items always get lost in standard corner cabinets, but many unique solutions, such as this pullout semicircular shelf, are available today from cabinet manufacturers.

Corner base cabinets are notorious for their deep, dark, difficult-to-reach corner space. If you're installing new cabinets, you can solve that problem by ordering units with revolving lazy susan shelves that provide easy access to any item.

You can retrofit existing cabinets with trays that pivot on a rod. Available at kitchen speciality stores and home centers, they're designed so that opening the cabinet door brings the items front and center. These units are sometimes called half-moon trays because of their shape.

Base cabinets often can accommodate new drawers. By combining large, deep drawers for skillets, woks, and other pots and pans with small drawers for utensils, potholders, and kitchen towels, a cook can have all the necessary implements readily at hand.

You can purchase or build rolling drawer inserts that fit behind closed cabinet doors; keeping the drawer fronts hidden gives a unified look to the cabinet fronts. However, you may prefer units that do not necessitate opening cabinet doors to pull out the drawer.

Drawers can hold tableware, as well as silverware, towels, and the usual kitchen utensils. Using drawer dividers keeps things in their correct places.

ORGANIZING LIDS

Lids for cookware always seem to roll around and get in the way of everything else you're storing in a cabinet.

Commercially available coated-wire lid hangers are easy to install. But here's a simple Saturday afternoon do-it-yourself project to solve that storage problem.

Build the sides of the racks from 1×3 pine. Cut the top and bottom edges to the design of your choice. Measure your lids

to decide what kind of spacing you need for the cross pieces, which you can cut out of ¾-inch square molding. Cut simple dadoes in the side pieces for the racks, glue and nail the racks, and finish the unit to match the cabinet door. Before you screw the entire unit to the inside of the base cabinet door, you will probably have to trim the interior shelves to make room for the rack when the door closes.

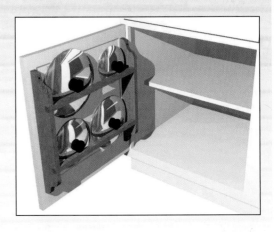

BUILDING A PULLOUT TRAY

With lumber and off-the-shelf hardware from your local home center and time for a one-day project, you can build and install this pullout tray.

If the sides of the cabinet are not flush with the inner edges of the face frames, you'll need to install a pair of ¾-inch cleats, onto which you can mount standard drawer slides. Check that the face of each cleat is flush with the face frame.

Glue and screw the cleats to the cabinet sides. Attach the drawer slides so that their top edges are ½ inch below the top edges of the cleats. Be sure the drawer slides are level from front to back and with each other. Once the hardware is in place, measure the width between the drawer slides and the depth of the cabinet to be sure the cabinet doors will close.

Build the tray as you would a drawer. Cut ¼-inch dadoes in the front and side plywood pieces to accommodate the plywood bottom. Assemble the tray with glue and 4d finish nails. The bottom edge of the back piece should be flush with the top of the dadoes in the side pieces to accommodate the tray bottom. Attach the pullout hardware to the sides. To install a second pullout tray, attach another pair of plywood cleats to the sides of the cabinet above the first pair.

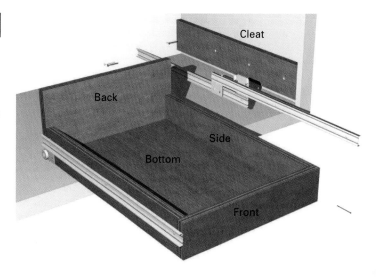

BUILD A PULLOUT ORGANIZER

You can nest pans and keep track of lids with an easy-to-build pullout organizer. If your cabinet is wide enough, install a ¾-inch plywood divider in the center to separate two organizers, one on each side. Cut the divider to the interior dimensions of the cabinet, then glue and toenail it into position.

Install the cleats and hardware in the sides of the cabinet as described for the tray above.

MATERIALS LIST

Item	Material	Dimensions	Qty
Sides	½" plywood	3×22"	2
Front	½" plywood	3×14"	1
Back	½" plywood	6×14"	1
Cleats	¾" plywood	4×22-24"	2
Bottom	¼" plywood	13×21"	1

4d finish nails; 1¼" #6 drywall screws; two 22" drawer slides; carpenter's glue; stain or paint.

With the hardware in place, measure the width and depth of the cabinet, allowing for the distance between the drawer slides. Make the organizer with a 6×14-inch front board. Cut ¼-inch dadoes for the bottom, as you would a drawer. Cut a 4-inch-diameter semicircular opening in the front board. Glue and nail the organizer with 4d finish nails. You can purchase a ready-made wire organizer to hold the pan lids.

MATERIALS LIST

Item	Material	Dimensions	Qty
Front	½" plywood	6×14"	1
Back	½" plywood	6×14"	1
Low Side	½" plywood	6×22"	1
Basket Side	½" plywood	18×22"	1
Cleats	¾" plywood	4×22-24"	2
Bottom	¼" plywood	14×22"	1

4d finish nails; 1¼" #6 drywall screws; two 22" drawer slides; one wire rack, about 10×18×4"; white carpenter's glue; wood putty; stain or paint.

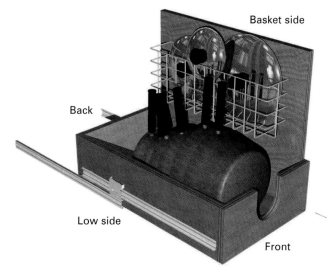

THE KITCHEN
continued

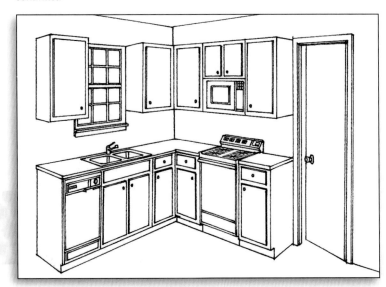

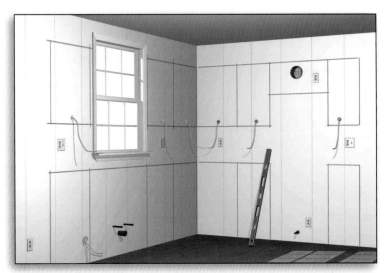

If you've analyzed your kitchen and concluded it's poorly organized, there's not enough storage space, you can't retrofit existing cabinets to meet your needs, or you want a style change, there's one solution left: Rip it out and start over.

That sounds intimidating, and many people use professional kitchen planners and installers to tackle such a job. But with careful planning and a helper or two, installing new cabinets is not beyond the reach of a determined do-it-yourselfer.

Measure your space carefully and plot out the room on graph paper. Sketch in your ideas of what you think should be where, taking into consideration the present location of doors, windows, and utilities.

Whether you order cabinets through a specialty supplier or the cabinet department at a home center, you probably will have access to their computer-aided design programs. They'll show you on a computer screen how various configurations will look. And when you're satisfied with the design, they'll print a drawing and materials list.

Once you've cleared out the old cabinets, mark the location of the wall studs on the walls and roughly draw in the locations of the cabinet units. While the kitchen is empty, take advantage of the opportunity to upgrade your electrical, plumbing, and ventilation systems if they need it. Make all your plumbing, electrical, gas, and heating, cooling, and ventilation rough-ins before you start to install any cabinets.

Do the installation in five steps: wall, base, corner, end, then peninsula or island cabinets.

INSTALLATION TIPS

■ Do you want the wall cabinets to extend all the way to the ceiling? Doing so will give you more storage space, but it's space that's hard to reach, suitable only for rarely used items. If you don't need the space, you might want to build soffits above the cabinets to create a clean look between the cabinets and the ceiling. Or you can leave the space open and top off the wall cabinets with crown molding. This space can then be used to display collectibles.

■ Although aesthetically pleasing when they match, wall and base cabinets need not be the same width.

■ Use corners effectively. Avoid blind corner cabinets if you can use L-shape cabinets fitted with revolving lazy susans.

■ Unless your kitchen is extremely small, expect at least a week of down time. Set up a temporary kitchen somewhere else in the house where you can cook meals with a microwave and do dishes in another sink.

■ Clear out as much of the old kitchen as you can before you start. Don't do your demolition, however, until you have a firm delivery date on your new cabinets.

■ Cabinets must be plumb and level

in all directions for the door hardware to be fitted and function properly. Make sure your floor is not out of level by more than about 2 inches. You can shim cabinets that much and use toe kicks and moldings to cover the gaps. Otherwise, level the floor by adding a plywood underlayment.

■ Fasten cabinets securely. Always fasten cabinets to the wall through the cabinet frames, not just the back. Wall cabinets must be screwed into wall studs. Anchors alone, driven into drywall or plaster, will not hold the heavy loads.

INSTALLING WALL CABINETS

Contractors differ on whether it's better to install base or wall cabinets first. Many find it easier to install wall cabinets first because the base cabinets are not in the way.

Wall cabinets are typically installed so their bottoms are 54 inches above the floor, allowing for 34-inch base cabinets, 2 inches for a countertop, and 18 inches between the counter and the bottom of the wall cabinet.

If you're going to install an appliance garage between the counter and wall cabinets, make sure it is designed for this 18-inch space.

Start in the corner where the floor is the highest. Measure up 54 inches from the floor and draw a level line to mark the bottom of the cabinets. Even if you install the temporary ledger strip, as shown below, you'll be glad if you have recruited someone to help you hold the cabinets in place as you install them.

Attach a temporary 1×3 or 2×4 ledger strip along the line you drew on the wall. Recheck that it is level and screw it into the wall studs you located earlier.

Set the first wall cabinet on the ledger strip. Check for level from front to back and side to side and for plumb. Install shims to correct problems. Secure the cabinet to the wall, driving 2½-inch screws through the top and bottom cabinet frames, through the shims, and into the wall studs.

Set the second cabinet next to the first and attach it loosely to the wall through the top framing piece. Clamp the cabinet faces together and check for level and plumb. Make sure the face frames are flush with each other. Drill countersunk pilot holes in the face frames and join the face frames with 2½-inch screws. Then finish securing the cabinet to the wall studs. Repeat for the rest of the run.

If your cabinets run from wall to wall, it's rare that they will fit exactly in the space. You'll probably have to install a spacer strip on the last cabinet. Rip the spacer to width and attach it to the last cabinet's face frame before you install that cabinet. The spacer does not have to be secured to the wall, as it does not support anything. Manufacturers include molding to cover gaps between the top of the cabinets and the ceiling or along the side if the cabinets do not end against a wall. Attach this trim to the cabinet, not the ceiling or wall, with finish nails.

THE KITCHEN
continued

INSTALLING BASE CABINETS

The same installation steps used for wall cabinets apply to base cabinets. Besides placing shims behind the cabinets to plumb them, you may need shims under and between cabinets to make sure that they are level from side to side and front to back and that the face frames align perfectly.

To top off base cabinets, you can buy premade tops or have a countertop specialist measure the space after you install the cabinets and then build a custom countertop.

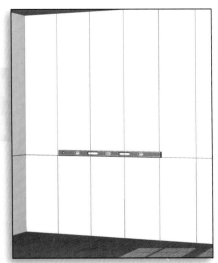

Again, begin at the highest point of the room and draw a level line at the height of the cabinet top. Remember, you can shim cabinets up but not down.

Set the first cabinet in place. Check for level from front to back and side to side and check the face frame for plumb. Insert shims where necessary to correct the alignment, then screw the cabinet to the wall studs with 2½-inch screws.

Set the next cabinet in place, level and plumb it, then clamp the face frames together. Make sure the frames are flush, then drill pilot holes and screw the face frames together. Check the level again and screw the cabinet to the wall studs.

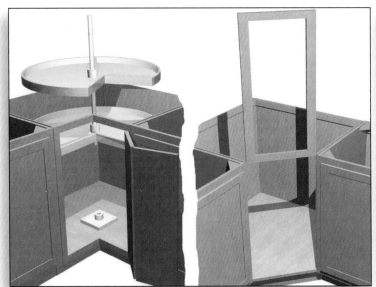

A corner cabinet may come as a complete unit that you install in one piece, or it may come in pieces that you need to assemble. Install complete units as you do other base cabinets, making sure that as you turn the corner the next run is also straight and level. Install sectional units according to the manufacturer's instructions. At the end of the run, install a wall spacer, if required.

Once the base cabinets are installed, you can add a toe-kick board that matches the cabinets or a vinyl cove base to hide any gaps between the cabinets and floor. Gaps at the top of the toe-kick board caused by out-of-level conditions will be hidden from view.

INSTALLING ISLAND AND PENINSULA CABINETS

If you need more storage space for pots and pans, plus an area for food preparation and dining, consider creating a peninsula or an island. In roughly 12 square feet of floor space, you can store baking supplies or additional cookware and have room on top to prepare meals or serve plates.

Although an island uses valuable floor space, it allows you to store conveniently items you are now crossing the kitchen to get. Islands with doors on more than one side are especially efficient and accessible.

The preferred clearance between an island and other counters or cabinets is 36 inches, but 30 inches or less might be comfortable in a kitchen with only one primary cook.

■ You can purchase a ready-made island or peninsula cabinet, or you can use a run of one or more standard base cabinets. In this case, you can cover the back side of the cabinets with finished veneer that matches the cabinets. When you do not need access to one side of the cabinets, you can make the countertop wider on the far side to serve as a stool-height dining area.

Islands and peninsulas should always be attached firmly to the floor. Measure the bottom inside dimension. Then screw 2×4 cleats to the floor so that the cabinet fits over the cleats tightly. Secure the cabinet to the cleats with screws or finish nails driven through the toe kick area into the cleats.

■ Don't forget the potential storage space that exists above an island or peninsula. Unless you're installing a range in the island or peninsula, in which case you'll need to install a range hood above it, the space is ideal for suspending cabinets from the ceiling. It's a great place to display prized china or collectibles behind glass-paneled doors.

Mounting island or peninsula cabinets on the ceiling uses the same procedure as for base

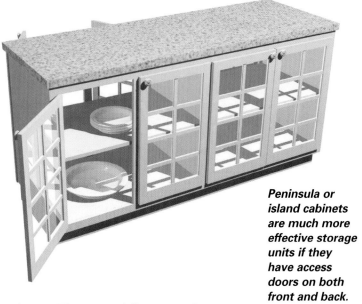

Peninsula or island cabinets are much more effective storage units if they have access doors on both front and back.

cabinets. The major difference is that you must be sure that the cleats you install on the ceiling are tied securely into the ceiling joists with at least 4-inch lag screws.

Another storage option above islands is a hanging rack from which to hang pots, pans, and other utensils.

To secure an island cabinet to the floor, turn the unit upside down and measure its inside frame. Screw

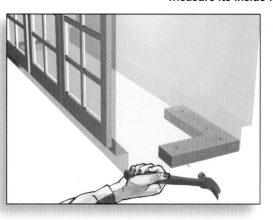

cleats on the floor according to those dimensions and place the cabinet over the cleats. Secure it to the cleats with finish nails (or screws if the unit has a kickspace where screws won't be noticeable).

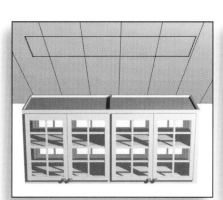

Ceiling-hung cabinets are installed in much the same way as an island base cabinet.

A critical step in anchoring a cabinet to the ceiling is to screw the cleats securely into the ceiling joists.

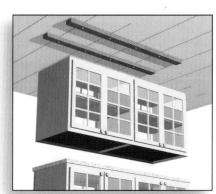

This isn't a one- or even two-person job. Make sure you have a couple of helpers when you raise the cabinet.

BATHROOMS

Bathrooms are pitiful underdogs in the storage contest. Rarely is one any match for the glut of linens, cosmetics, cleaning supplies, and the health and hygiene products all vying for space.

The average medicine cabinet offers a Band Aide solution to an "E.R." crisis. It just doesn't measure up to the needs of most families. Little space for linens, supplies, and cleaners, which you'll want close at hand, compounds the problem.

Style also plays an important role in the bathroom. No matter how much countertop space you have on your vanity, you probably aren't eager to load it up with personal supplies, especially if the bathroom serves guests as well as family.

Out-of-sight storage usually is limited to wall cabinets and vanity base cabinets. But most vanity cabinets are shells that don't take advantage of their volume of space. You can benefit from a little planning and ready-made

Using wall space is critical in bathrooms. The open format of this bathroom lends itself to the between-the-studs open shelves that serve as both storage and display space.

or build-it-yourself upgrades. It's in the bathroom that you also need to look at using walls, door surfaces, and corners and nooks for your storage needs.

Scope out areas near the bathroom, too, such as an adjacent hallway or bedroom closet, for storage of occasionally used items.

EXPAND THE MEDICINE CABINET

The typical home medicine cabinet bulges with pharmaceutical miracles and day-to-day staples. If yours is stuffed like a grocery bag, and you've exhausted the entertainment value of family skirmishes over who gets what on which shelf, it may be time to replace your old vanity. Even if you have a single-sink vanity, you may be able to mount a wider medicine cabinet over it without the larger mirror and cabinet visually overpowering the sink and vanity.

Medicine cabinets come in two styles: those that fit into the wall cavity and those that mount directly on and extend out from the wall. Some have built-in lights; others have separate lighting kits.

Most are relatively easy do-it-yourself jobs. If you have a recessed unit, the biggest challenge in the changeover may be removing the old cabinet.

Take advantage of a wall cavity in your bathroom. A built-in cabinet stores towels and hides all the hair dryers, curlers, and other toiletries that a busy family needs.

MAKE BETTER USE OF VANITY SPACE

A quick peek inside most vanities shows a chaotic mixture of personal-care and cleaning products, usually strewn across a single bottom shelf. If you're replacing a vanity, consider one that has multiple or roll-out shelves. That makes it easier to get to those seldom-used items that now hide in the shadows at the back of the vanity. You can retrofit an existing vanity using the idea on page 38 or by adapting the kitchen cabinet roll-out drawer plan on page 31.

USE READY-MADE PRODUCTS

From a variety of towel racks to shower caddies that hold soap, shampoo, and wash clothes, to wire baskets and mobile carts, countless products can help you add storage to the nooks and corners of your bathroom.

Again, it's a matter of style and of the amount of space available in the bathroom.

If you don't mind having items out in the open, you'll be able to choose from an endless array of accessories. On the other hand, if you like everything stored in its proper place and you have the floor space, don't hesitate to consider furniture. For example, a small chest of drawers that complements your bathroom style can be an extremely functional storage option. And plenty of mobile carts can provide either open or closed bins or baskets.

The medicine cabinet, shelves, or built-in storage must take the place of vanities if your bathroom has a charming old— or modern— pedestal sink.

If you don't mind having a few things out in the open, consider freestanding shelving in the bathroom. This wood-and-glass unit is a graceful solution for towel storage.

BATHROOMS

continued

MAXIMIZING THE VANITY

You can retrofit many styles of vanities to accommodate a roll-out drawer. An advantage of such a drawer is not having to lean far into the cabinet to retrieve something near the back—the back becomes the middle when you roll it out. Consider building a narrow, high shelf at the rear of the unit. By double-decking the space, you'll have room to separate towels and washcloths from personal-care items. Be sure to design the shelf around the sink bowl, trap, and water supply valves, which share this space. Attach the shelf with nails or screws and glue, making sure to predrill holes so you won't split the wood. Also be sure to use the type of drawer glides that permit the whole unit to be removed easily so you can get at the plumbing.

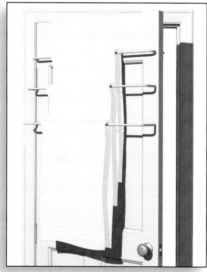

STORING TOWELS: Storing bath towels where you need them means finding room in the bathroom, rather than down the hall. Open shelving above the toilet can put clean towels and tissues within easy reach. A door-hinge towel rack makes perfect use of otherwise underused space behind the door and doubles as a robe or clothing hook. Other towel racks mount directly on the walls or on the insides of doors. Children especially will appreciate the low towel rack on either of the multilevel rack systems illustrated here.

USING THE WALLS: Most bathroom walls serve few functions other than holding towel racks. You can put them to good use by converting the spaces between the wall studs to open storage for bath items, toiletries, or personal appliances, such as hair dryers or razors. If you have fears of tearing into your walls, you can work outward, simply using the bookcase building techniques you learned in the first chapter to build shelves. The space above the toilet is a particularly good location for such a shelf system.

BUILDING A THROUGH-THE-WALL, TWO-SIDED CLOSET

If you have sufficient wall space in the bathroom and an adjoining room, consider building a cabinet between the studs into the adjoining room. This through-the-wall cabinet can serve both rooms. The cabinet shown here uses the depth of the stud wall, usually about 5 inches, plus an 11-inch extension into the next room. With a total depth of 16 inches, you can have 8-inch-deep bookshelves on one side and 8-inch-deep bathroom shelves for washcloths and toiletries on the other.

The design uses the entire depth of the top shelf on the bathroom side for towels only. The bottom shelf on the bedroom side will be full depth to the wall, perfect for storing one or two pairs of shoes.

Begin by checking the bathroom wall and the adjoining room for electrical wiring, pipes, and shear bracing. Locate the studs where you want to install the cabinet. Open the wall by cutting the drywall or plaster with a keyhole saw. Use a straightedge to mark a straight line along the stud and remove the wall material up to the stud with a cleancut line. If you encounter fire blocking, remove it and relocate it above and below the location of the cabinet.

Unless you intend to paint the cabinet, use cabinet-grade plywood. Rip the plywood to 16 inches, then cut two sides 78 inches long. Make a cutout 5 inches deep and 18 inches long on the bottom of each side to accommodate the wall. Cut a toe kick 3 inches deep and 4 inches high on the bedroom side. At the top, cut a rabbet $\frac{1}{4}$ inch deep and $\frac{3}{4}$ inch wide. Lay out dadoes, $\frac{1}{4}$ inch deep and $\frac{3}{4}$ inch wide, 13 inches apart in each side for the shelves. Before you cut the dadoes, make sure they line up exactly.

Cut the shelves $13\frac{1}{2}$ inches long to allow for the rabbet and dadoes.

To accommodate the $\frac{1}{4}$-inch plywood partitions between the bedroom and bathroom sides, cut $\frac{1}{4}$-inch dadoes $\frac{1}{4}$ inch deep and 8 inches in from the same edge of the cabinet sides and the shelves.

Assemble the shelves with 6d finish nails and glue. Apply construction adhesive to the studs, then insert the unit into the wall and screw the sides of it to the wall studs. If you leave the shelves open, veneer tape can be ironed onto the plywood edges. If desired, you can add the optional face frame and doors. Consider using two doors—upper and lower—rather than a single long door.

MATERIALS LIST

Item	Material	Dimensions	Qty
Sides	$\frac{3}{4}$" plywood	16×78"	2
Top	$\frac{3}{4}$" plywood	$13\frac{1}{2}$×16"	1
Bottom	$\frac{3}{4}$" plywood	$13\frac{1}{2}$×16"	1
Shelves	$\frac{3}{4}$" plywood	$13\frac{1}{2}$×16"	4
Partitions	$\frac{1}{4}$" plywood	$13\frac{1}{2}$×$14\frac{1}{2}$"	4
Face stiles	solid birch	$\frac{3}{4}$×2×64"	2
Face rails	solid birch	$\frac{3}{4}$×2×$18\frac{1}{2}$"	3
Doors	$\frac{3}{4}$" plywood	$15\frac{1}{4}$×$29\frac{1}{2}$"	2

6d finish nails, 2" #8 drywall screws, four cabinet hinges, birch veneer, carpenter's glue, wood putty, construction adhesive, paint or oil, as needed.

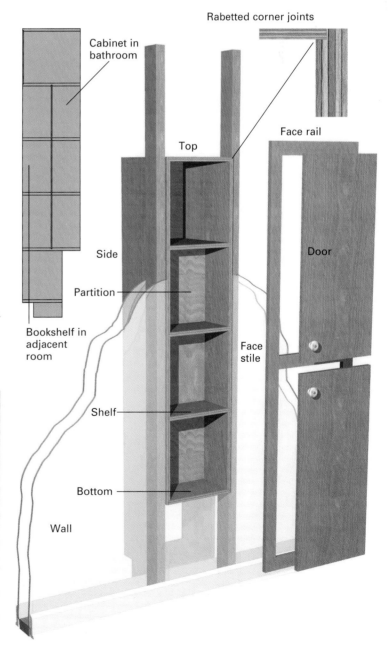

Cabinet in bathroom

Rabbetted corner joints

Top

Face rail

Side

Partition

Door

Bookshelf in adjacent room

Face stile

Shelf

Bottom

Wall

LAUNDRY AND UTILITY ROOMS

Laundry, ironing, and cleaning supplies usually find their way into closets, drawers, cabinets, and corners throughout your home. In many instances, this is good because you probably are storing everyday cleaning supplies close to where you use them—kitchen linens and sink cleaners in the kitchen, bathroom linens and porcelain cleaners in bathroom, and brooms, mops, and vacuums near their areas of use. If cleaning items are not handy, it's all too easy to skip those cleaning chores.

You will, however, want to set aside some dedicated storage space in your home to store cleaning supplies that are used only occasionally or those toxic ones you need to keep out of reach of children or pets. If you're lucky, you have a utility room or extra space in the laundry room that can serve as a storage area for all these items.

Standard kitchen cabinetry is an easy solution if you have room to install it in a laundry or utility area. Cabinets with roll-out or tip-down bins work well as clothes hampers in the laundry center. Open storage cubicles or cabinets can handle work and play coats, raincoats, shoes and boots, and sports equipment. A variety of hooks and other hanging gadgets make storing these items even easier.

If you don't have a separate room in which you can implement these ideas, you can adapt them to the other potential storage areas throughout the house that you identified in your initial storage planning.

You don't need a big space to have a laundry room. Modern space-saving washers and dryers, fold-down ironing boards, and wire clothes hampers make this area work efficiently.

Claim space at the rear entry for coats and hats, shoes and boots, and outdoor toys. You'll save the rest of the house from kiddie clutter.

MAKE ROOM FOR RECYCLING

As more and more towns and cities develop recycling programs, you as a homeowner have to find a spot to sort cans, bottles, newspapers, and other recyclable material. A convenient arrangement of bins and organizers makes this job easier.

If your municipal program requires a special curbside container, try to work it into your design. Or you may prefer a series of bins in the utility room or kitchen that you empty into the curbside container weekly.

One solution is to retrofit base cabinets with ready-made accessories. If you can spare 3 to 4 feet of base cabinet, for example, you could set up four stacked bins on a track that could be pulled out individually on wheeled drawers. Another solution is a frame that holds a plastic bin inside the base cabinet door. There are also cabinets available that have pullout or tilt-out bins already installed, either side by side or in pairs, one behind the other.

CLEANING UP

Many ready-made products are available to keep brooms and mops orderly. These can be mounted easily in closets or pantries. It's also easy to make your own cleats on the wall from wood blocks, used dowels, or sewing thread spools. A wall surface covered with perforated hardboard, equipped with hangers, offers another alternative for brooms and mops. Storage for your vacuum should be built into a closet near where you use it most.

If you have sufficient space in a utility room, you can install a standard kitchen pantry cabinet in which you can modify the shelving to serve as your storage headquarters for mops, brooms, and cleaning solutions. In this way you can store hazardous items on high shelves and have everyday items handy below them.

Another solution for storing cleaning supplies is a variation on the between-the-studs storage space shown on page 38.
■ Carefully cut out the drywall or plaster between two wall studs.
■ Mount a plywood frame and shelves inside the cutout area. You might use perforated hardboard as the frame back.
■ Then repair the wall around your new unit. If you wish, you can cut doors from ½-inch plywood and hang them from simple hinges set on the face of the plywood frame.

Cabinetmakers have come to the aid of utility rooms. False-drawer, pullout trash bins are popular. This homeowner left the drawer unit out of one cabinet section and ordered a panelless door to provide a protected space for the family cat's litter box.

Recycling fits your lifestyle better when you have a place to stash everything. This recycling center was built in a pantry.

Keep cleaning supplies neat and handy under the kitchen sink with a pull-down, false-front tray and slide-out wire rack.

LAUNDRY AND UTILITY ROOMS
continued

BUILDING A FOLD-DOWN IRONING CENTER

A stow-away ironing board is there when you want it and out of the way the rest of the time. This project is an attractive alternative to costly commercial products.

A fold-down ironing-board unit can be installed in a tall cabinet made out of ¾-inch plywood (*similar to the bookcase described on pages 18-19*). The outer dimensions of the cabinet are 25½×74×9¼ inches, large enough to stow the ironing board with space left for a stack of narrow shelves to hold your iron and other supplies.

■ Cut the ironing board from ¾-inch plywood or a length of 1×16. Use an old ironing board as a template.

■ Cut a 15⅞-inch length of closet pole and attach it to the board with two 1¼-inch conduit straps. Fasten the straps 8¼ inches apart with screws.

■ Rip two 24-inch lengths of 1×10 to 8¾ inches. Using the end of the closet pole, draw three circles on each piece. Connect the circles to form the figure-7 shape shown.

■ Cut around the marked shape with a jigsaw, taking care that the resulting slot is wide enough to allow the closet pole to slide without binding.

■ Screw the slotted panels to the inside of the cabinet. The top of the figure 7 establishes the top of the ironing board; standard height ranges from 32 to 35 inches, depending on the height that suits you.

■ To make the brace board, cut a length of 1×8 to 43 inches. Bevel one end to about 15 degrees; this end will be attached to the bottom of the cabinet. From the 1×8 cut a small shelf 14 inches wide.

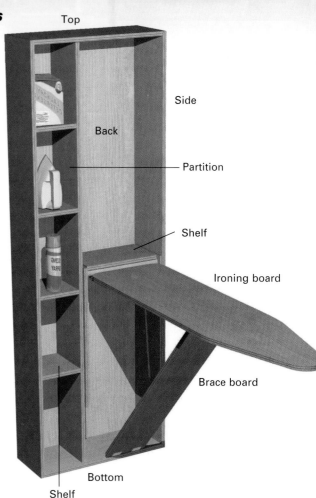

Top

Side

Back

Partition

Shelf

Ironing board

Brace board

Bottom

Shelf

MATERIALS LIST

Item	Material	Dimensions	Qty
Back	¼" plywood	25×73¼"	1
Sides	¾" plywood	9¼×74"	2
Top	¾" plywood	9¼×24¾"	1
Bottom	¾" plywood	9¼×24¾"	1
Partition	¾" plywood	9×73"	1
Shelves	¾" plywood	9×8"	4
Ironing board	¾" plywood	14×54"	1
Brace board	1×8 pine	43"	1
Pivot	1¼" closet pole	15⅞"	1
Connectors	1¼" conduit straps		2
Slotted boards	1×10 pine	8¾×24"	2
Small shelf	1×8 pine	14"	1
Cleat	1×2 pine	16"	1
Wedges	1×2 pine	4"	2

Two 1×2" hinges, three 2×2" hinges, magnetic catch, 1½" #8 roundheaded wood screws.

■ Attach a 1×2 cleat across the back of the cabinet between the two slotted boards so the top edge is at the same height as the top of the figure 7. Fasten the shelf to the cleat using two 1×2 hinges. Holding the shelf in the up position, lift the ironing board assembly into place. The back should be supported in the figure-7 slots and the front should rest on the floor.

■ Lower the shelf onto the closet pole and mark the position for the two small wedges on the bottom of the shelf. Cut wedges from a piece of 1×2 and attach them to the bottom of the shelf outside of the conduit straps. These wedges will keep the closet pole in position when the ironing board is in use.

■ Attach the three 2×2 hinges to the brace board before installing it. While a helper holds the ironing board level, set the brace board in place and mark the hinge locations on the cabinet floor and the ironing board. Attach the top hinge first.

■ Finally, attach a magnetic latch to the folding shelf and cabinet back. This holds the shelf in the up position.

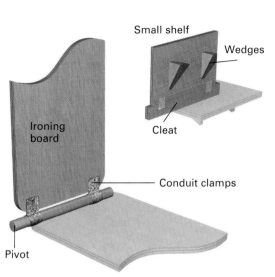

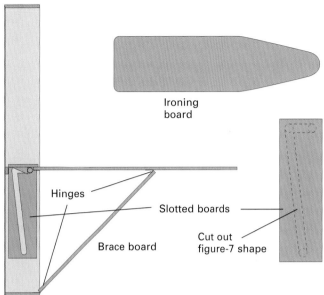

BUILDING AN ABOVE-THE-WASHER STORAGE UNIT

Even if your laundry area has barely enough space for a washer and dryer, you can build a simple cabinet and shelf storage system to help keep the area organized. This project is designed to fit in the approximate 60-inch width of a washer and dryer. Adapt the dimensions to the space you have available. It consists of a standard kitchen wall cabinet on one side to store items out of sight, a set of open, ready-made shelves on the other side to store items within easy reach, and a closet pole in between to hang your clothes as you remove them from the dryer.

First, locate the wall studs and mark their locations. You'll want to anchor the cabinet and shelves into the studs. Hang a standard 24-inch kitchen cabinet on whichever side of the arrangement you prefer (*see page 33*). If you have a top-loading washer, make sure you hang it high enough above the washer that the door will open.

For the shelves, buy ready-made, laminate-covered shelves. Support the top shelf with three shelf brackets: Two closet-rod-type supports are installed next to the cabinet and in the middle next to the shelves; the third support on the end of the shelf can be a simple utility-shelf bracket. Suspend closet pole from the two brackets.

Mount the other shelf supports to the wall at the height you choose, depending on the items you will store on the shelf. Using the ready-made units, there's no finishing to do.

MATERIALS LIST

Item	Material	Dimensions	Qty
Cabinet	Standard kitchen cabinet	24×30×12"	1
Clothes rod	1¼" closet pole	21"	1
Top shelf	¾" laminated particleboard	12×36"	1
Lower shelves	¾" laminated particleboard	12×18"	2

Two shelf supports with closet rod brackets, five utility style shelf supports; 2½" drywall screws, appropriate wall anchors and screws.

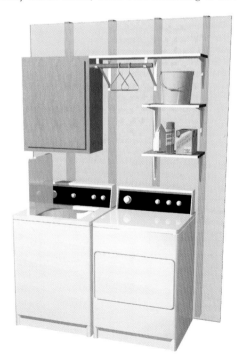

Make use of wall space for storage in bedrooms. At the gable end of this attic room, dual built-in closets and shelves flank a window seat over a blanket chest.

BEDROOMS AND CLOSETS

It's human nature: People horde more stuff than they have space in which to keep it. The tycoon with a vast bedroom suite could use one more jewelry chest; the restless vagabond could use a bigger knapsack.

Bedrooms tend to force the storage issue. We can try to ignore clutter deep in the basement, but bedroom storage—now there's a problem we have to sleep with. Bedroom closets get stuffed with wardrobes that expand and change: winter and summer clothes; clothes that fit now and others that surely will (again).

In the master bedroom, you may need to find space for reading, sewing, and ironing or even a corner for a home office.

Children's rooms get buried in toys, games, and hobby gear. Older children may lose their homework center under piles of clothing. They need space for books, perhaps a computer, and other school supplies.

Guest bedrooms are chameleons; their appearance can change at any time. If guests are infrequent, this space can be disguised as a home office, sewing center, study hall, or catch-all storage for seasonal wardrobes.

If your bedroom space is at a premium, concentrate first on the closet. In this chapter, we take a look at using walls effectively, taming the closet, and organizing children's rooms. If your bedroom will include an office or sewing center, you'll find more ideas in later chapters.

IN THIS SECTION

Making Effective Use Of Bedroom Walls **46**

Taming the Closet **47**

Seasonal Storage Options **52**

Lining a Closet with Aromatic Cedar **53**

Storage Solutions in Children's Rooms **54**

MAKING EFFECTIVE USE OF BEDROOM WALLS

USING A WALL SYSTEM

Demand more from your walls than just a flat surface for displaying artwork and photographs. Wall storage systems can hold books, personal files and records, electronic equipment, sewing supplies, and just about anything else you're willing to keep in sight. And units with drawers can stash things you don't care to look at, including clothes—which takes a load off shelves in the closet or drawer space in dressers.

Wall systems don't have to be exotic built-in units. Freestanding, ready-made or kit systems can help you back your storage problems up against the wall.

USING ARMOIRES OR DRESSERS

Conventional dressers and armoires can store items other than socks, underwear, and lingerie. Make room for sweaters, casual slacks, and seasonal clothes to free up space that these items might take up in your closet. Most armoires provide room for hanging clothes and can help you ease the squeeze in your closet.

Boxes, bins, and interior shelves will help you take advantage of your armoire's full capacity. Shelves and cubbyholes allow you to store more without reducing your convenient access to individual items.

SLEEPING LIKE HOUDINI

Wouldn't it be great if that big old guest bed would just disappear when you don't need it? You can perform this magic—and it's no illusion. For extremely small or cramped bedrooms or for your guest room, consider a hide-a-bed, or Murphy bed, as they often are called. Hide-a-beds can be purchased as freestanding units, as built-ins, or as sofas. Combined with a freestanding bookcase or wall storage system, they can transform a bedroom wall into a highly efficient storage system. And when the hide-a-bed is folded up, the space is available for that sewing center or home office you wished you had room for.

TAMING THE CLOSET

The common closet could scarcely be more spartan: a single rod for hangers, a single shelf above it, maybe a bare light bulb. The builders must have been kidding, right? Let's get serious: It's time to divide and conquer with a system that divides that closet into spaces just right for clothes, shoes, linens, and storage boxes.

Begin organizing each closet by listing all the things you would like to keep in it. Use the basic storage concepts outlined in the first chapter: Separate the items by logical categories and by how often they are used—often, occasionally, or seldom. If an item is used only once or twice a year, banish it into exile elsewhere.

Decide how much space you need for hanging items, for shelves, storage boxes, shoes, and what needs to be on hooks or in drawers. If possible, add an extra 20 percent for future purchases.

Divide hanging clothes into sizes, grouped according to the family member, then by vertical measurements. Allow enough horizontal room in your measurements so the items are not crowded.

Estimate shelf space needs by stacking linens, sweaters, and storage boxes, then taking measurements. Try to use multiple shelves with 7–12 inches of vertical space so you won't have to stack items in tall piles. Consider buying attractive plastic storage boxes, then make the shelf space at least 2 inches taller than the boxes.

Keep everything off the floor for ease of cleaning. Shoes are a common source of clutter. Shoe racks, shelves, or hanging bags keep them off the floor and within easy reach.

Use hooks sparingly. They often are awkward and make clothes appear untidy. If you use them for robes, belts, or ties, locate them on the back of the closet door or off to the side of the closet. A section of drawers in the closet is handy, especially if you don't have a dresser in the bedroom.

Closets generally are 22–24 inches deep; shelf units are 16–20 inches deep. Building wooden shelves, the least expensive alternative, takes time and labor, especially in the finishing and painting steps.

Alternatively, many kit closet systems are available at home centers or specialty storage stores. These are easy to assemble but will cost more than lumber. You may not get the perfect fit for your closet. Sometimes a combination approach works best: Construct simple shelves yourself and fit store-bought units into that basic skeleton.

ACCESSORIES

Men's ties 27"
Garment bags 60"
Travel dress bags 50"
Travel shirt bags 41"
Hanging shoe bag 38-60"
Umbrellas 36"
Bare hangers 17-20"

MEN'S CLOTHING

Topcoats 50"

Suits 40"

Slacks, cuff-hung 44"

Slacks, double-hung 30"

Shirts 35"

WOMEN'S CLOTHING

Suits 40"

Coats 52-55"

Dresses 50"

Long dress 68"

Shorts, cuff hung 28"

Robes 52-55"

Blouses 34"

Skirts 38"

TAMING THE CLOSET
continued

OFF-THE-SHELF SOLUTIONS

Amazing, isn't it, how big a closet looks on paper? Wire storage systems take advantage of every inch. A plan like this will help to boost your closet's performance. Install a system that fits, then take control by refilling that space wisely.

Walk into any home center, speciality storage store, or even a discount department store and you can find a wide variety of ready-to-assemble closet storage systems. They're designed for installation by the average homeowner. Some units, especially shelves, can be cut to fit your space; others, especially drawer sections, cannot be sized to fit.

Shelf and rod units are a good place to start. They can be adjusted up or down to use space effectively, and a variety of drawer and shelf units are available to mix with the rod and shelf units.

You'll find two basic styles of ready-made or kit closet storage systems: ones made of wood components and those of plastic-coated wire grids. The wire-grid systems allow for greater ventilation and almost never need to be dusted. On the other hand, they cannot hold small items, such as jewelry, and they do not hide items, such as underwear, that you may prefer not to have visible. Using plastic slide-out baskets instead of wire ones can solve the first problem, but most of those components are made of clear plastic, which does not solve the second problem.

No matter which system you select, take careful measurements of your closet, plan the space requirements you need (*use the clothing measurements on page 47*), then sketch your ideal solution on graph paper. With your plan in hand, your retailer can assist you in selecting the proper components and installation hardware. Many stores also supply do-it-yourself installation guides; others, especially the specialty storage stores, offer detailed planning and installation services.

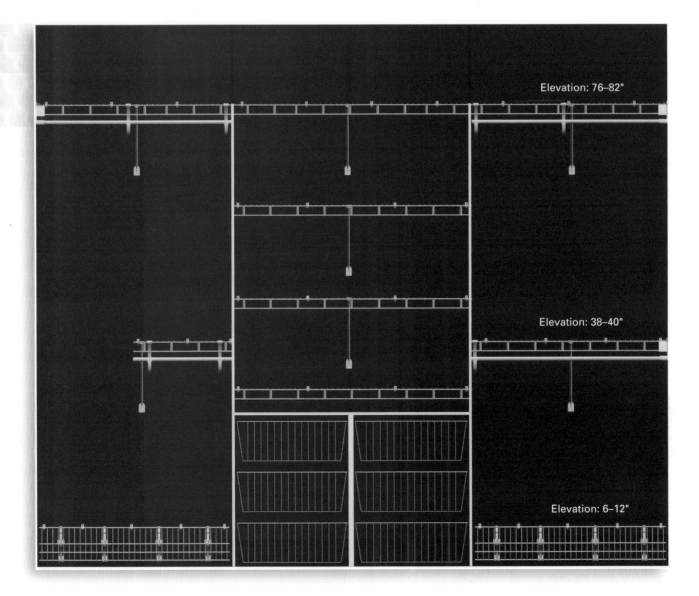

Elevation: 76–82"

Elevation: 38–40"

Elevation: 6–12"

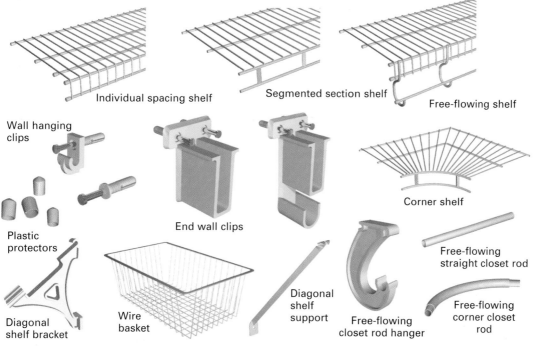

Individual spacing shelf

Segmented section shelf

Free-flowing shelf

Wall hanging clips

Plastic protectors

End wall clips

Corner shelf

Diagonal shelf bracket

Wire basket

Diagonal shelf support

Free-flowing closet rod hanger

Free-flowing straight closet rod

Free-flowing corner closet rod

Most wire-grid closet systems are similar, but manufacturers have distinct brackets and mounting clips, as well as three basic styles of front edges on shelves: individual spacing, segmented, and free-flowing. Basket units can be freestanding or attached to vertical support rods.

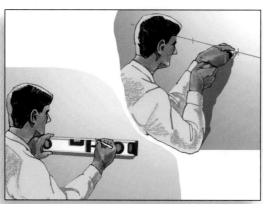

Using a level, draw a level line at the desired height. Locate studs and attach the wall mounting clips to the studs with screws. Between studs, use the appropriate wall anchors. Depending on the system, the shelves snap or hook onto the clips.

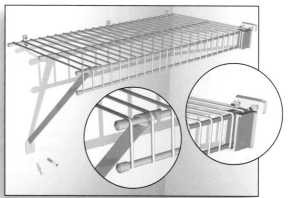

Install wall brackets to hold the end of the shelf where it meets the wall. You probably won't hit a stud here, so use appropriate wall anchors. In the middle of spans, you'll need to attach diagonal shelf supports according to the manufacturer's directions.

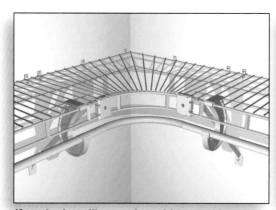

If you're installing a wire-grid system in a walk-in closet, corner shelf units connect shelves on adjacent walls. These are attached in the same manner as straight shelves, with clips on the back side and diagonal braces where the sections meet.

This shoe rack is a regular straight shelf, inverted so the front lip is facing up to hold the shoes on the slanted surface. Special triangular support brackets mount on the wall to hold the shoe rack in place.

TAMING THE CLOSET
continued

BUILDING YOUR OWN CLOSET SOLUTIONS

For a little money and not that much work, you can build this basic shelf-and-rod closet system out of two sheets of plywood. The design shown here is for a basic 8-foot-wide by 2-foot-deep closet with bifold doors.

You can adapt it as you want and as your carpentry expertise allows. After cataloging your clothes, for example, you may find you need more than the 18-inch width for dresses and other long apparel on one side. Or you may to want two sections of stacked shelves, one for her and one for him.

Begin by ripping the two sheets of plywood into six 14-inch-wide pieces. Plan and mark out all the pieces to length on these strips. Cut out all the pieces and paint or stain them before beginning assembly.

On the side pieces of the upright shelf unit, mark the location of the shelves based on your calculations of what type of clothes or linens will be stored on them. Because clothing does not weigh much, you can do without dado cuts or cleats and use simple butt joints for these shelves. Again, if you have the skills and inclination, you could use dado joints or substitute adjustable shelf supports to make these shelves movable.

Assemble the upright shelf unit with nails or screws. You can assemble it outside the closet if you're sure it will go through the closet door after assembly. Before setting the unit into the closet, glue and screw 1×2 cleats to the bottom of the highest shelf and the second-to-lowest shelf, making sure the flat side of the 1×2 is flush with the back edge of the shelf. Set the unit tight against the back of the closet, removing any molding at the floor or notching the unit so it fits around the molding. Make sure the unit is in position and plumb, then attach it to the wall by driving screws through the two 1×2 cleats into the wall studs.

Once the upright shelf unit is in place, draw level lines on the unit and the closet walls to indicate where the remaining shelves go. Cut additional 1×2 cleats to attach the back edge of each shelf to the wall as well as to the side wall of the closet and the upright shelf unit. Attach these cleats, then set the shelves on the cleats, securing them with nails or screws driven down through the top of the shelves into the cleats.

MATERIALS LIST

Item	Material	Dimensions	Qty
Sides	¾" plywood	14×83"	2
Top shelf	¾" plywood	14×96"	1
Mid shelf	¾" plywood	14×60"	1
Unit shelves	¾" plywood	14×16⅞"	7
Shoe shelves	¾" plywood	15×17⅝"	2
Clothes rod	1¼" closet pole	60"	2
Clothes rod	1¼" closet pole	17⅝"	1
Cleats	1×2 pine	60"	2
Cleats	1×2 pine	13"	8
Cleats	1×2 pine	16⅞"	2
Heel stops	1×1 pine	4"	2
Trim	¾" molding	30'	

3d, 6d, and 8d finish nails; 2¼" #8 drywall screws; six 1¼" closet-rod rosettes; two shelf supports with closet-rod holders; white carpenter's glue; wood putty; paint or stain.

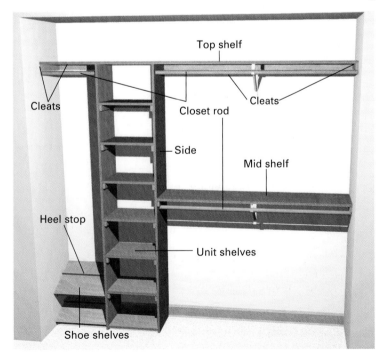

Top shelf

Cleats

Closet rod

Cleats

Side

Mid shelf

Heel stop

Unit shelves

Shoe shelves

For heel stops on the shoe-rack shelves, cut pieces of 1×1 the same length as the shelf. Attach them about 5 inches from the back of the shelf, or use your own shoes to calculate the best distance. Install the shoe shelves so they slope upward to the back.

Install the clothes rods with closet-pole holders, called *rosettes*. You probably won't hit studs on the side wall, so use the appropriate wall anchors. Because the rods are longer than 4 feet, you will need to reinforce them in the center with a shelf support fitted with a closet-rod holder.

Attach ¾-inch trim molding to all visible edges. Set all nails and fill the holes with wood putty. Paint the edges to match the shelves and touch up any paint you may have marred during installation.

ALTER SHELVES FOR YOUR NEEDS

There are several ways you can alter the upright shelf unit to adapt it to your needs. Here are three ideas:

■ Cut dadoes in the side pieces and install shelf standards so the shelves are adjustable.
■ If you're handy and want to build a couple of drawers, install drawer slides in some of the shelf cavities.
■ Use wire baskets as drawers. In this case, cut a ¼-inch dado groove at the correct height for the basket slide and simply slide the basket into the shelf unit.

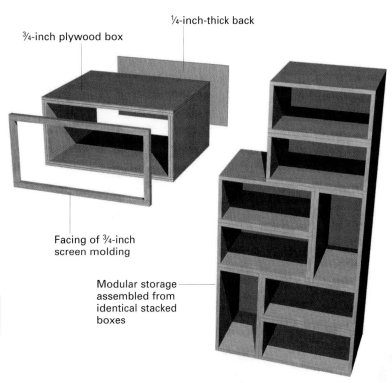

¾-inch plywood box
¼-inch-thick back

Facing of ¾-inch screen molding

Modular storage assembled from identical stacked boxes

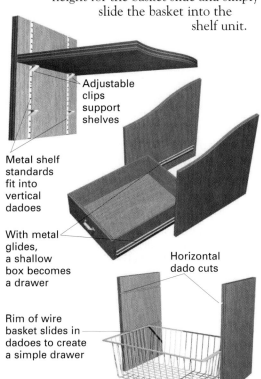

Adjustable clips support shelves

Metal shelf standards fit into vertical dadoes

With metal glides, a shallow box becomes a drawer

Horizontal dado cuts

Rim of wire basket slides in dadoes to create a simple drawer

REACHING HEIGHTS OF STACKABLE STORAGE

If you think you may change your storage plan in the future, stay flexible by using stackable boxes that can be moved easily from one room or closet to another. There are plenty of ready-made boxes in stores, but building a set is as simple as building a basic box (*see page 17*).

As with the preceding closet project, if you rip plywood sheets into three equal widths, you'll wind up with 16-inch-deep boxes, a convenient size for most clothes and closets. Plywood works well, and it's hard to find dimension lumber wider than 11¼ inches.

The suggested dimensions allow you to build eight 19¾×16×9⅞ boxes out of two sheets of plywood. Cut eight short pieces out of one of the ripped lengths and eight long pieces out of the other lengths. After cutting, you'll find it easier to paint or stain the interior surfaces before assembling the boxes.

Prior to nailing the butt joints together, apply glue to each joint. Put them together with 6d finish nails. To provide rigidity and keep the boxes square, cut backs for the boxes out of ¼-inch hardboard, attaching each with 4d finish nails. To give the boxes a finished appearance and minimize the risk of splinters, trim the front edges of the boxes with ¾-inch screen molding, applied with glue and 3d finish nails.

SEASONAL STORAGE OPTIONS

If you've organized your closets and used your wall space efficiently and still do not have enough space, it's time to take stock. First, are some of your clothes expendable? If you haven't worn something for more than a year, it's fodder for a garage sale or a donation to a clothing charity.

Next, take stock of those seasonal items: Shorts and short-sleeved shirts just get in your way in winter, and bulky sweaters take up space in the summer. The hassle of moving such items twice a year is more than offset by the space gained in your closets and dressers.

Seasonal clothing can be stored in a dry basement or attic in stackable boxes or on a clothes rod. Because they may be stored for several months, such items should be sealed from dust and insects. Plastic storage boxes are an easy solution for foldable items. Sturdy, stackable containers eliminate the need for shelving. For hanging clothes, heavy-duty garment bags zip closed.

Wool and some other fabrics need to be stored in mothproof places. Although mothballs and cedar chunks repel these pests, they can leave a strong odor in clothes. The best solution is to have clothes dry-cleaned, then zip them in a plastic garment bag. As an alternative, large cardboard boxes with hanging rods are available from moving companies at reasonable prices. Although the boxes do not have especially tight seals, they keep most of the dust out of your clothing, are relatively stable, and last a long time if not moved around too often.

Don't ignore unique solutions for storing seasonal items. If you find that perfect antique chest or trunk at an auction, it'll be a great place to keep sweaters in the summer and shorts and swimwear in the winter.

Other commercial products— plastic bins, garment bags, or the moving companies' big cardboard boxes with hanging rods—serve as useful storage for seasonal items.

LINING A CLOSET WITH AROMATIC CEDAR

Surrounding your clothes with cedar is a refreshing way to protect them. While not always 100 percent effective, aromatic cedar does repel moths and other insects. It also helps prevent mildew. And cedar looks and smells great.

Cedar boards used for decks and other applications do not have the aromatic and pest-control qualities needed for closets. Aromatic cedar is more expensive, but manufacturers have come up with ways to make a little cedar go a long way. It is available in ¼-inch-thick tongue-and-groove boards or in 4×8-foot panels that have a cover layer of cedar chips. The panels are less expensive, easier to install, and just as aromatic as the boards.

Either product can be installed over open studs, if you're building a new closet, or over drywall or plaster in an existing closet. If there is mildew in the closet, wash the affected area with a bleach solution (one part bleach to four parts water) before installing the cedar. If the closet is prone to dampness, correct the problem before putting up the cedar. For instance, you can install sheets of rigid foam insulation and a plastic vapor barrier before you add the cedar.

Boards and paneling can bridge holes and gaps in closet walls, but they cannot hide major misalignments. Straighten out any large problems on the walls before you begin.

If you're installing cedar boards in a closet, mark the location of the studs on the wall. If you're using paneling, mark the stud locations on the floor and ceiling at each end of the studs.

To install horizontal boards, begin at the bottom of the wall and work upward. Using hard trim nails, which are thinner than regular finish nails, face-nail the bottom row. Nail the rest of the rows on the tongues only, driving one nail at each stud. Butt joints need not fall on the studs; the tongue-and-groove at the ends of each piece will hold them in place. Avoid butt joints within 1 inch of the butt joint directly above or below it.

To install paneling, cut the paneling to fit. Don't bother trying to make precise cuts for out-of-square corners; gaps will be covered by trim later. Apply paneling adhesive to the back of the paneling in a regular pattern of squiggles. Press the panel in place and nail it into the studs with light brown paneling nails. Add trim to cover the corner gaps.

Aromatic cedar should be left unfinished. After two or three years, if the cedar has developed a hard surface and is no longer aromatic, sand it lightly and that fresh, spicy aroma will come right back.

Whether you build it from scratch or line an existing closet, whether you use cedar panels or tongue-and-groove cedar boards, there's nothing like the aromatic freshness and beauty of a cedar-lined clothes closet.

STORAGE SOLUTIONS IN CHILDREN'S ROOMS

Children's rooms house an inherent conflict: You want to keep a lid on chaos, but you also want to allow your kids to be kids. Storage solutions will work in children's rooms only if they are easy to use.

Making units easy to use depends partly on the ages of the children. Especially in closets of young children, you may have to think horizontally, rather than vertically, so items are easy to grab and, more importantly, easy to put away.

Young children don't need the same kind of ordered storage that adults or teenagers do. A box into which they can toss toys can suffice. A lid on it to hide the jumble should satisfy your yearning for a neat-looking room.

As children grow older, they'll require more and more shelf space to handle board games, puzzles, trophies, hobby and sports equipment, and books.

Well-managed hooks can be helpful in children's rooms. But every hook should be designated for a specific purpose—sports gear, school bags, jackets, or other clothing. Children tend to generalize hooks as catch-alls, testing the hook's load tolerance and their parents' general tolerance.

Use the same approach to planning a child's room as in other spaces in your home. Inventory the type and number of items that need to be stored, then plan accordingly, taking into account the size of the child and easy access to belongings.

In this child's walk-in closet, in-season clothes are kept at a reachable height; out-of-season stuff gets stashed up high.

Built-ins, such as a loft-bed with dresser storage beneath it or a study center with plenty of drawers work well in cramped kids' rooms.

BUILDING A TOY CHEST

Anyone with basic carpentry skills who can make straight, clean cuts will enjoy building this attractive chest. A power miter saw or radial arm saw makes the process easier, but a simple backsaw and hand miter box and a circular saw with a rip guide will work just as well. The rounded brass hardware is not only decorative, it also prevents damage to corners and reduces injuries to toppling toddlers.

To build this chest you'll need grade A, select, tongue-and-groove fir flooring for the front, back, ends, and lid. The brace and end pieces use grade A or B select 1×4s.

Begin by cutting all the wood pieces to length. Miter cut the ends of the braces at 45 degrees so there will be no sharp edges inside the chest. Rip-cut the four boards for the top on the sides, front, and back to remove the tongue portion of the boards. Temporarily assemble the strips for the lid, then measure and rip-cut the front and back pieces so the lid is 22 inches wide.

Assemble the strips for the front, back, ends, and lid. Use a framing square to make sure the units are square. Position the inside braces to allow clearance for the adjacent pieces. Space the braces evenly across each of the surfaces. The end braces on the front and back should be spaced in from the edge of the front or back the width of the end panels so

that when the end panels are attached, the braces serve as cleats to reinforce the corner butt joint. Attach the braces with glue and 3d finish nails. Assemble the lid in the same way, attaching the braces ⅞ inch from the edges.

Attach the ends to the front and back with glue and 6d finish nails. Use glue and 3d finish nails to attach the base 1×2 to the plywood bottom, keeping the good side of the plywood up. Slip the chest over the base unit, then glue and screw it on. As an option, you could attach casters to the 1×2s on the base so the unit would be mobile.

Set all the nails, fill the nail holes with wood putty, and paint or varnish the chest. After the finish has dried, secure the lid to the chest with a piano hinge. Attach and adjust the lid supports and install the handles and corner protectors with the fasteners provided with the hardware.

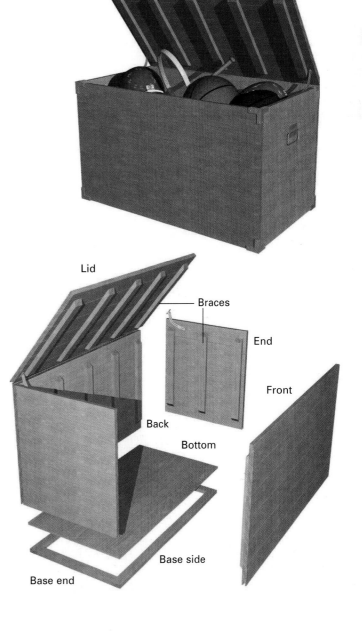

MATERIALS LIST

Item	Material	Dimensions	Qty
Front and back pieces	1×4 tongue-and-grove flooring grade-A select	40"	12
End pieces	1×4 T&G, *as above*	20½"	12
Lid pieces	1×4 T&G, *as above*	40"	7
Inside braces	1×2 fir, grade A or B select	15¼"	16
Lid braces	1×2 fir, *as above*	20¼"	5
Base sides	1×2 fir, *as above*	38½"	2
Base ends	1×2 fir, *as above*	17"	2
Bottom	½" A-D ply	20½×38½"	1

3d and 6d finish nails; 1½" #6 drywall screws; two brass adjustable-tension lid supports; one 40" brass piano hinge; two brass handles; 12 brass corners; white carpenter's glue; wood putty; paint or varnish.

Lid

Braces

End

Front

Back

Bottom

Base side

Base end

STORAGE SOLUTIONS IN CHILDREN'S ROOMS

continued

BUILDING A LOFT BED

Two kids sharing a bedroom—even one child squeezed in a small room—can test your skill at managing floor space. Bunk beds are the traditional answer. But if you're a veteran of college dorm life, you probably already know of another solution—the loft bed. Raising the bed off the floor frees that space for many other uses.

Loft beds can be of many designs, supported by any combination of posts and wall-hung wooden braces, called *ledgers*. Lofts should be designed carefully with good supports because, as the nursery rhyme says, "there will be monkeys jumping on the bed."

BED SIZE: The loft shown here is designed for a twin-size mattress. Check your mattress dimensions before you build, and modify the specifications as needed. This simple structure can be built in a day. But with modifications, the bed can be as complex as you want. Its height should be determined by the age of your child as well as the ceiling height. Strive for 50–60 inches off the floor so you have plenty of space underneath, but make sure you provide comfortable head room above.

Start by cutting the side and end supports to length. Cut a rabbet 1 inch wide and ¾ inch deep along the inside top edge of all the supports. Make a level line at the height of the two ledgers, then find wall studs and mark their location. Temporarily nail the ledgers to the wall and predrill holes through the ledgers into the studs. Drill countersunk holes for the lag-screw heads, then screw the ledgers to the wall, making sure the rabbeted edge faces to the inside of the bed. Drive a screw into every wall stud for security.

Lay the 4×4 corner post and 2×4 ladder rail next to each other and mark the spacing for the ladder rungs. Space the rungs about 8 inches apart. Using a 1¼-inch spade bit, drill ½-inch-deep holes for the rungs.

SECURITY: Cut 1½-inch-wide by 3½-inch-deep rabbets on the adjacent outside edge of the top of the post. Predrill countersunk holes in the outside and end supports, then lag-screw the supports to the post. Lag-screw the front side support to the end of the short ledger; hang the end side support from a joist hanger on the long wall ledger. For extra security, add a 2×4 post under the short ledger and front side support. Screw this to the wall with appropriate wall anchors because you probably will not be screwing into a wall stud. Equally space the three 2×4 supports between

You may be designing a loft bed to solve a space problem or to give your child a fun place to sleep. Involve the kids in the planning phase so they can share in the sense of achievement when it is finished.

TAKE ADVANTAGE OF NEW SPACE

You probably had some ideas for that new space when you planned on installing a loft bed. Are these ideas on your list?

■ Place a regular bed under the loft. Place the bed parallel with the loft and you duplicate a bunk-bed situation but use all the space you created. But if you place the lower bed perpendicular to the top one, you'll still have an empty space alongside that bed.

■ Make a homework center under the loft. You can buy a premade student desk, or add two more ledgers to the wall at an appropriate desk height for your child. Then install a plywood panel (24–30 inches wide) on the ledgers and add a corner post as you did for the loft. Cover the plywood with ⅛-inch hardboard and you'll have a hard, smooth work surface for homework or hobbies.

■ Build shelves at the post-end of the bed between the wall and the corner post. Shelves could face either outward, inward, or both.

■ The space under the loft makes good dresser space. You can place the dresser, rather than shelves, at the post end.

the ledgers and install them with joist hangers, making sure their tops are even with the bottom of the rabbet in the side supports. The plywood bed board sits in the rabbet.

Cut a 1½-inch-wide, 3½-inch-deep rabbet on the outside top edge of the ladder rail. Set the rail under the side support, apply glue to

MATERIALS LIST

Item	Material	Dimensions	Qty
Side supports	2×6 pine	78"	2
End supports	2×6 pine	37"	2
Middle joists	2×4 pine	37"	3
Corner post	4×4 pine	58¾"	1
End post	2×4 pine	54"	1
Bed board	¾" plywood	77×39"	1
Ladder rail	2×4 pine	58¾"	1
Ladder rungs	1¼" closet rod	20"	6

2×4 joist hangers; 3" lag screws; 6d and 8d nails; 2½" drywall screws; white carpenter's glue; paint or varnish, as needed

the rung holes in both the post and rail, insert the rungs, and push the ladder unit together. Screw the ladder rail to the side bed support from the back side. Paint or stain the bed to match the decor of the room.

If the loft is for a young child, you can add a railing around the top bedframe. Prebuild a rail and baluster system and screw it to the 2×6 supports. You'll have to leave a gap for access to the ladder. Remember that balusters should never be farther apart than 4 inches so a child's head cannot be caught between them.

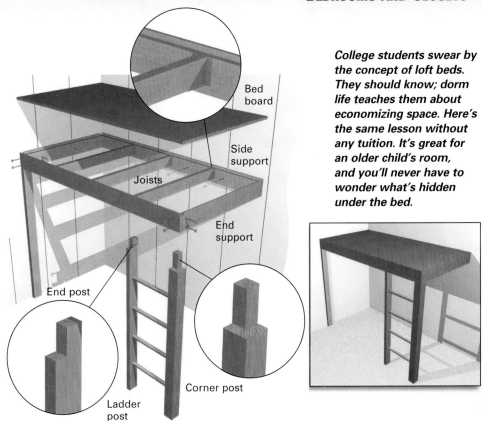

College students swear by the concept of loft beds. They should know; dorm life teaches them about economizing space. Here's the same lesson without any tuition. It's great for an older child's room, and you'll never have to wonder what's hidden under the bed.

BUILDING AN UNDER-THE-BED ROLL-OUT DRAWER

The area under the average bed, where you usually find dust and missing socks, can be maximized for storage. You can buy many ready-made trays designed to fit in this space. Or you can build this simple roll-out one to the size you need.

Make these units no more than 3 feet wide, especially if they will contain heavy objects. Wider ones will sag and be cumbersome to pull out and push in.

Construct a simple frame using 1×4s or 1×6s. Cut a rabbet into the bottom edge of the boards to accommodate a ½-inch plywood bottom. Use a jigsaw to cut handle openings on one or more sides. Sand all the pieces, then join the corners with glue and 6d finish nails.

For a simple box without casters, give the bottom several coats of high-gloss paint or polyurethane so it will slide easily. If you want casters, attach 2×2 rails to the sides of each unit, then attach the casters to the rails. They should extend at least 1 inch below the rails to ensure adequate clearance, especially if floors are carpeted.

You also can add a hinged plywood or hardboard lid to keep dust out of the box. But this will make access to the items awkward because you will have to pull the unit all the way out from under the bed to open it. If the roll-out is for seasonal or rarely used items, however, a lid is a good choice.

There are 20–30 square feet of good storage space under conventional beds. Put that space to good use by building mobile trays to store toys, games, linens, or items you don't use regularly.

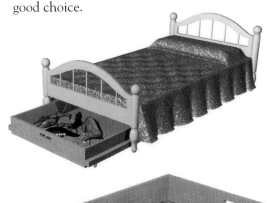

How you use your living and working areas determines the type of storage space they need. Take an assessment of your lifestyle before you plan storage alternatives.

ABOVE: *In this formal living room, space is allocated to display of art and collectibles.*

FAR RIGHT: *In a less formal family room, an entertainment center becomes a focal point.*

RIGHT: *Baskets filled with flowers and shelves brimming with collectibles lend comfort, charm, and order to a cottage living room.*

LIVING AND WORKING AREAS

Out-of-control clutter is a private problem in your basement or attic. But entryways and living rooms put the problem on public display. Add home offices and hobby rooms, and you quickly realize that you can't hide your storage woes. In these very visible activity centers of your home, things can pile up quickly. Coats, boots, mail, school papers—no wonder it's sometimes hard to find the cordless phone or the television's remote control.

Compounding the problem is the fact that these living areas often lack closets. You can find some help in furnishings: coffee or end tables with internal storage, baskets for mail or magazines, umbrella stands and coat racks. But for major storage relief, look to your walls to provide space for bookcases and cabinets.

Your lifestyle as well as your decorating style will affect your storage choices. If you reserve the living room for formal entertaining, you may choose not to have any storage in it at all. But in a casual family room or office, open shelves may be an ideal solution.

This chapter examines organizing entryways and hallways, then delves into making effective use of wall spaces in formal and informal rooms. The remainder of the chapter suggests ideas for organizing home offices, workshops, and hobby areas so your free-time activities are more pleasurable.

IN THIS SECTION

Entries and Hallways **60**
Formal Living Rooms **62**
Family Rooms and Great Rooms **64**
Dining Rooms **66**
Home Offices **70**
Workshops and Hobby Centers **73**

ENTRIES AND HALLWAYS

A formal entry provides a stand for umbrellas and a tabletop where you can set parcels and keys while you hang up your coat. Such storage provisions are decorative, as well as functional.

Your parents warned you to stay out of the way of traffic. That warning applies to home storage as well. Entries and hallways are high-traffic areas where clutter can be a hazard as well as an eyesore. You need to provide space for outerwear, such as coats, hats, shoes, boots, and umbrellas. You should also have a temporary place to set down shopping bags, mail, purses, briefcases, or school bags.

An organized entryway closet is the best solution. Use the principles outlined in the previous chapter and the ideas on the next page to improve your closet's performance. But remember that your entry closet may be used by more than one age group, so make sure that the low storage space is allocated for children and higher space for adults.

If your entryway lacks a closet, consider a coat rack or, if there's wall space, a row for hooks. These are ideal in back entries for work and play coats and sports equipment.

Besides furniture and specialized storage stores, your search for ideas can include flea markets, garage sales, and thrift shops:

■ Old milk cans make great umbrella stands.

■ A steamer trunk or hope chest in the hallway can store hats, mittens, and other winter wear.

■ A small cafe table can provide a *temporary* set-down spot for magazines and mail.

■ If your entry hall is wide enough, a wall shelf system will hold these items, while providing a place to display collectibles.

An informal back-door entryway could be a jumble of kids' junk if their parents didn't provide this orderly storage system.

BUILDING A HALLWAY SHELF

A shelf near the most-used door of your house can hold keys, mail, and the other items you lug in each day. Add some Shaker pegs below it, and you have a convenient place to hang light coats, hats, or umbrellas.

The shelf shown here is 30 inches wide, but you can make it any size. Cut the top shelf to length, round the corners with a jigsaw, then sand the edges smooth. Cut another 1×12 13 inches long, then draw the pattern illustrated to cut two knee braces. They should be at least 12 inches long so you have enough room for two countersunk holes for the screws to attach the shelf to the wall studs. Notch the back of the braces to accommodate the 1×6 cleat that holds up the back of the shelf and holds the Shaker pegs.

Drill holes the size of the pegs you purchase, placing one peg on the outside of each brace and two equally paced between the braces.

Space the braces 16 inches apart so you can secure them to wall studs. There's no need to assemble the unit before you attach it to the wall. But it's a good idea to sand and paint or stain the pieces before assembly.

MATERIALS LIST

Item	Material	Length	Qty
Top shelf	1×12 pine	30"	1
Cleat	1×6 pine	28"	1
Knee braces	1×12 pine	13"	2

Three Shaker-style pegs; 2½" #8 drywall screws; 6d finish nails; wood putty; paint or stain as desired

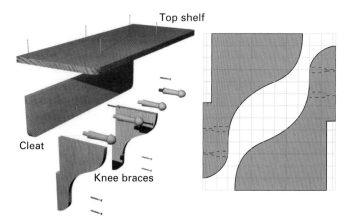

Top shelf

Cleat

Knee braces

ORGANIZING AN ENTRY CLOSET

Most entryway closets are small, with room for just a few coats on a rod and a shelf above it. Increasing the usable space calls for carefully organizing the closet along the lines of the bedroom makeover shown on page 50. If the closet has sufficient space above the existing shelf, add a second shelf for storing seldom-used items.

Another solution is to use stackable boxes *(see page 51)*. The boxes can be sized to hold shoes, boots, purses, briefcases, camera equipment, hats and mittens, or whatever you need to keep handy as you leave the house.

MAKE A SHOE SHELF

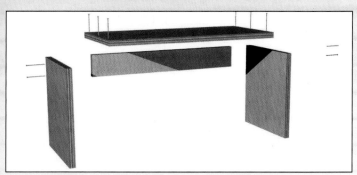

Make use of the space beneath hanging coats. Here's a simple shelf for shoes and boots that you can build in less than 2 hours. All you need for a 24-inch-wide closet is a 4-foot 1×12 and a 2-foot 1×4. Cut the sides 12 inches high and make the back cleat 1½ inches shorter than the top shelf so it fits under the shelf between the sides. Assemble with glue and 6d finish nails.

FORMAL LIVING ROOMS

A repeating arch over cabinet doors and shelving raises interest in this handsome wall of storage, built into a formal living room. Decorative treasures and favorite books grace the open shelves. The cabinets hide occasionally used tableware and linens for the adjoining dining room.

Because the living room usually is the most formal space in the house, the style you set for the room may well dictate what kind of storage systems you employ. A painted plywood unit might be suitable for a family room or den, but the living room may require something with finer craftsmanship and finishing. Thus, your best options in a living room are fine furniture items or built-in units planned and built by a professional woodworker.

Finding storage spaces in a formal room requires the careful planning outlined in the first chapter. Analyze the traffic pattern and furniture placement, then look for unused wall spaces away from these areas. Take advantage of spaces alongside a fireplace, in the corners of the room, under or beside windows, or on walls with no windows.

If you don't have a separate family room, you'll need to make some compromises. For example, if you want a formal look but still need to have your television, videotape recorder, and music systems within easy access, you can build or purchase an entertainment system cabinet that closes up to hide all the equipment when not in use.

Evaluating your entertainment habits helps you plan how best to use the living room space. If you have separate family and living rooms, you'll want to divide the entertainment activities, and their associated storage requirements, between the rooms—for example, television viewing in one and reading or listening to music in the other.

Fireplaces are natural focal points, so a fireplace wall often offers opportunities for storing and displaying books and collectibles.

Concealing items behind cabinet doors can dress up an informal living space when the occasion dictates.

MAKING YOUR OWN NICHE

Storage isn't limited to everyday items that we need readily at hand. Mementoes, collectibles, and works of art deserve special places of their own. Your living room may provide an ideal place to display such an item in this arched wall niche. With patience, a minimum of materials, and basic skills, you can build it in a weekend. Complete the final taping and texturing in a few evenings, and you'll have an architectural feature that you'll be as proud of as you are of its contents.

The niche is designed to fit in the space between two wall studs, 14½ inches apart. Establish the baseline of the niche, then find the studs by carefully cutting away the drywall or plaster to locate the studs. Mark the wall with vertical lines. Find out exactly how deep the niche can be by slipping a ruler into one of the holes you cut.

The key to making the niche look as if it were professionally crafted is taking plenty of time to apply and smooth the final coats of drywall compound. Blend the new material to the texture of the existing wall.

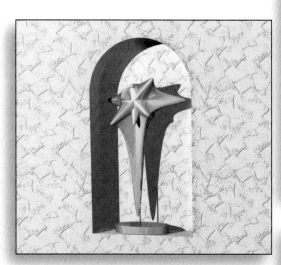

MATERIALS LIST

Item	Material	Size	Qty
Arch strips	Matte board	Varies	6–8
Cleats	1×4 pine	6"	2
Blocking	2×4 pine	14-15"	2
Bottom	Drywall	4×14"	1

1½" #6 drywall screws; 6d box nails; paneling adhesive; white carpenter's glue; 8 feet of flexible drywall corner bead; drywall tape and compound; paint

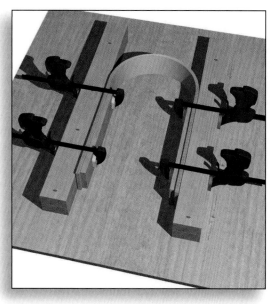

Construct a jig of plywood and 2×4s spaced as far apart as the distance between the studs. Cut six to eight strips of matte board the width of the arch. Build up the layers by laminating the strips with glue and sandwiching them between clamps and your layout form.

After drying, trace the outline of the arch on the wall. Cut the opening carefully with a utility knife or drywall saw so you won't have to do a lot of wall patching. Install two cleats and 2×4 blocking to support the bottom of the arch. Place blocking at the top, also.

Secure the arch in the opening with paneling adhesive and add a piece of drywall on top of the bottom blocking. Cover the outer edge with flexible corner bead and the inside corners with drywall tape. Apply drywall compound, sand smooth, and paint to match the wall.

FAMILY ROOMS AND GREAT ROOMS

Family rooms rival kitchens as the centers of American households. With all the activity here, look to using wall spaces that are out of the traffic flow, as with the wall system in the photo at right.

Analyzing your entertainment habits is even more important here than in a formal living room. Are the components of an entertainment center the most important focus of this room? Are hobby activities the most important? Is it the hub of noisy activity, a quiet place to read, or both?

The projects described here are informal in style, but you can dress them up by using good-quality hardwoods.

Display and functionality are central to this storage cabinet in a family dining area.

This informal shelf unit is designed to hold nearly all types of music components with a standard width of about 17 inches. Check the sizes of your equipment and adjust the dimensions, if necessary.

BUILDING AN INFORMAL MUSIC SHELF UNIT

The top, middle, and bottom shelves of this music component rack are fixed to give it rigidity. The other shelves rest on adjustable hardware. While the unit is meant to be informal, be sure to select an attractive variety of solid wood that you can finish to match other pieces of furniture in your family room. Oak and birch are good choices.

Trim the fixed shelves with 1×2, leaving the lip on the top side. Use eight of the uprights to assemble the four corner units. To ensure these are flush, clamp the boards together and drill pilot holes. Then apply glue and drive 6d nails into the holes.

The top fixed shelf fits flush with the top of the unit; the bottom shelf fits 7⅜ inches from the bottom to accommodate the kickplates; and the middle shelf can be placed anywhere you want it.

Install these three shelves into the four corner units with glue and 6d nails.

Cut and install the metal shelf standards on four of the remaining side uprights. Make sure the slots and screw holes in the standards align on opposite sides. Install the side uprights to the three fixed shelves with glue and nails. Install the kickplates by driving screws from the inside into the uprights.

The plywood back adds rigidity. You could leave it off by adding two more uprights to stabilize the back side.

Before cutting and assembling the five adjustable shelves, check the interior dimensions of the unit to be sure the shelves will clear the metal shelf standards.

Back   Fixed shelves   Uprights   Movable shelves   Shelf trim   Kickplates

MATERIALS LIST

Item	Material	Size	Qty
Uprights	1×3s	72"	11
Fixed shelves	¾" plywood	16½×20½"	3
Movable shelves	¾" plywood	16×20"	5
Shelf trim	1×2s	varies	24
Front kickplate	1×8	22"	1
Side kickplates	1×8	17¼"	2
Back	¼" plywood	23×72"	1

Metal shelf standards and clips, 6d finish nails, white carpenter's glue, wood putty, stain or varnish

BUILDING AN INTERLOCKING SHELF SYSTEM

If you don't like long rows of books that must be propped up with bookends, consider a shelf unit that uses interlocking boards. In addition to books, it can store audio and video tapes or compact discs or display collectibles.

PREPARATION: From a sheet of ¾-inch plywood, rip three boards 12¼ inches wide. From these, cut the two end pieces 71¼ inches long and the top and bottom, each 47 inches long. Make a ¼-inch-deep, ⅜-inch-wide rabbet along the backside of each of these boards for the plywood back.

In the top, side, and bottom boards, cut ⅜-inch-deep dadoes for the other uprights and the shelves. For the cube system shown, these should be equally spaced.

Rip six other boards 12 inches wide. From these, cut three 70½-inch uprights and five 47-inch shelves. Carefully lay out the ¾-inch interlocking slots in each of these boards. Cut the slots 6 inches deep using a ¾-inch dado blade or a router bit. Dry-fit to make sure the face pieces are flush.

AN INSIDE TIP: Working inside the cubicles will be difficult after they're assembled, so fill holes and sand the boards before you put the unit together. You may want to apply a finish at this point.

ASSEMBLY: Assemble the outside frame with glue and 6d finish nails. Lay the frame on its front edge and glue and nail the back into the rabbet, making sure the unit is square. Flip the unit over and insert the vertical uprights into the dadoes with the slots facing outward. Slide the horizontal

shelves into the slots of the vertical uprights, applying glue to each joint.

Build the base unit, installing corner brackets to add stability. Attach it with glue and nails or use additional corner brackets and screw it to the bottom shelf from underneath. Apply veneer tape to the edges of the plywood. Then apply your final finish.

You can adapt the design of this interlocking shelf unit to create an entertainment center by making the shelves deeper (typically 16 inches) and varying the size of the cubbyholes. If you double the size of some, cut dadoes on one side of the respective uprights or shelves instead of cutting the interlocking slots.

MATERIALS LIST

Item	Material	Dimensions	Qty
Top, bottom	¾" plywood	12¼×47"	2
Sides	¾" plywood	12¼×71¼"	2
Vertical dividers	¾" plywood	12×70½"	3
Shelves	¾" plywood	12×47"	5
Back	¼" plywood	47×72"	1
Base front, back	1×4 pine	47¾"	2
Base sides	1×4 pine	12¼"	2

6d finish nails; corner reinforcing brackets; veneer tape; carpenter's glue; wood putty; stain or varnish

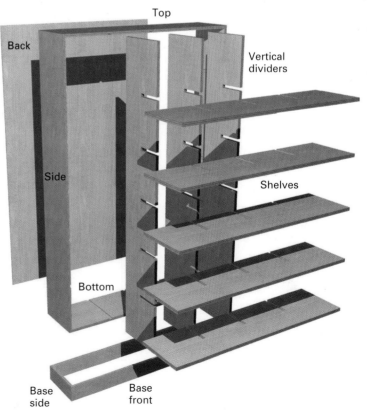

Back

Top

Side

Vertical dividers

Shelves

Bottom

Shelves

Base side

Base front

DINING ROOMS

Formal dining rooms tend to favor formal storage solutions: closets, buffets, and china cabinets. Less formal dining spaces adapt readily to more casual solutions, including open shelving, which can be created from commercial kits or from do-it-yourself plans.

Either approach helps to provide convenient places for silverware, china, linens, centerpieces, and the large trays and bowls required for food service.

You may want open or glass-fronted shelves to display fine china or dinnerware. And you'll probably favor cabinets with solid doors for more utilitarian pieces.

Many families use dining tables for homework, hobbies, puzzles, and games. If your dining room does such double duty, it will need extra storage space for books, games, photo albums, or maybe even a home office.

Here are some ideas and projects to help you get more comfort and enjoyment from these spaces. The projects on pages 68 and 69 can be adapted to living and family rooms by varying the materials and finishes to fit the style of the room.

ABOVE: *A classic dining sideboard can display cherished china and hold yards of linens and tableware in its doors and drawers below.*

A cafe-style booth, such as this breakfast nook, can swallow enormous amounts of gear under its bench seats.

If your formal dining room is serving Sunday dinners and taking most of the week off, put it to work as a home office in its slack hours.

BUILDING A SIDEBOARD

You can make this simple yet elegant sideboard using a standard kitchen wall cabinet. The 12-inch depth is perfect for storing plates and bowls, glasses and stemware, and linens. And it does not intrude into the room as would base cabinets, which are twice as wide.

TWO ADDITIONS: Making the cabinet into a sideboard requires adding only two items:
- An attractive and durable top.
- A recessed and elevating toe kick.

The toe kick enables the door to open easily and raises the cabinet off the floor so the shelves are more accessible.

For the top, buy cabinet-grade ¾-inch plywood that matches the cabinet's wood species (or that can be stained and finished to match). Apply veneer edging, fill holes, sand smooth, and apply the matching finish. Attach the top to the cabinet using #6 screws, driving them from inside the cabinet up into the plywood.

An alternative is to use solid wood of the correct variety for the top. But, unless you find a plank 13 or 14 inches wide, you would have to edge-glue two pieces together, which complicates the project.

TWO METHODS: There are two ways to make the toe kick:
- Here, we show cutting 4-inch strips of the same cabinet-grade plywood you used for the top. Build a simple box frame, making sure to reinforce the corners with wood block braces or metal corner angles. Use simple butt joints at the rear corners, but make 45-degree miter joints for the front corners. Sand and finish the toe kick as you did the top.
- Alternatively, many cabinet manufacturers make ⅛-inch-thick toe-kick trim that matches the cabinet finish. If you use it, make the frame out of 1×4 pine strips, then glue and nail on the trim strips. Attach the toe-kick unit by screwing #8 screws through the bottom of the cabinet into the frame.

MATERIALS LIST

Item	Material	Size	Qty
Cabinet	wall cabinets	12×30×36"	2
Top	¾" plywood	13×74"	1
Toe kick front	¾" plywood	4×66"	1
Toe kick back	¾" plywood	4×64½"	1
Toe kick sides	¾" plywood	4×9"	2
Toe kick brace	¾" plywood	4×7½"	1

Cabinet toe-kick trim; veneer tape; 3d and 6d finish nails; 1¼" #6 and 1½" #8 drywall screws; white carpenter's glue; stain or varnish

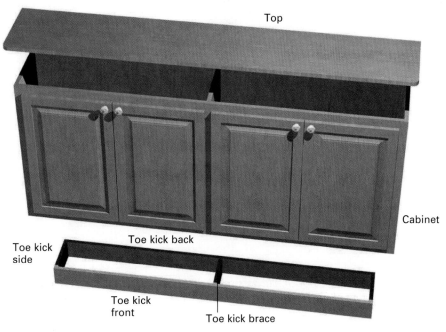

Top

Cabinet

Toe kick side

Toe kick back

Toe kick front

Toe kick brace

DINING ROOMS
continued

BUILDING A CORNER CABINET

Your search for storage space can explore every corner. Here's an attractive unit that can add many square feet of storage or display space. It can become a china cabinet in the dining room, a display case in the living room, or a bookcase in your den.

PLAYING THE ANGLES: Wedged into a corner, this open-front unit is perfect for storing books and mementos. Adding doors can make it suitable for holding any number of items, from pots and pans to clothing. Add glass inserts to the doors and you have a beautiful china cabinet.

The shelves are $19\frac{3}{8}$ inches at the deepest point, a greater span than normal for dimension lumber. Unless you are proficient at edge-gluing boards, it's best to use plywood for the shelves and the top and bottom pieces. You can make the face frame and rear spine out of solid wood.

From $\frac{3}{4}$-inch cabinet-grade plywood or solid 1-inch-thick pine or hardwood boards, rip two $5\frac{1}{2}$-inch-wide strips for the side pieces. Determine the desired height of the cabinet (72 inches is comfortable), then cut two $5\frac{1}{2}$-inch strips to that length. Next rip a

COMBINING WALL AND BASE CABINETS

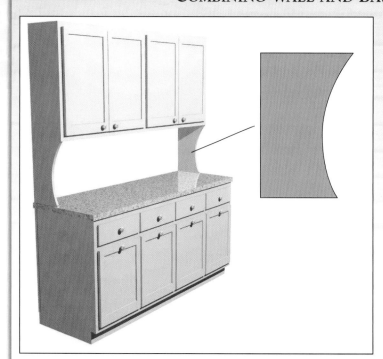

If you have sufficient floor area in which you can use standard 24-inch-wide base cabinets, here's an idea. Attach standard base and wall cabinet units to the wall studs. To make it look like a hutch, connect the two units with knee braces made out of matching wood, creating your own curved, angled, or straight design on the front of the brace. You also can fill in the back of the open space with matching wood to emphasize the look of a one-piece hutch. The brace is for looks only. Don't try to support the upper wall cabinet with it; mount that cabinet to the wall studs. In the dining room you probably won't want a plastic laminate countertop on the base unit. A butcher block, ceramic tile, granite, or slate top would be more attractive.

You can use this idea in rooms other than the dining room. For example, you could install a small sink in one of the base cabinets and a refrigerator in the adjoining units and have a setup for a wet bar in the family room or game room.

45-degree rabbet along the back edge of each side piece. Crosscut a ¼-inch-deep and ¾-inch-wide rabbet at the inner top of each side piece.

Butt the backs of the two side pieces against each other, with the inside faces up. Lay out your desired shelf plan on the inside faces, then cut a ¾-inch-wide dado in each side piece for each shelf. Be sure the facing dadoes line up with each other so the shelves will be level.

Cut a 2×4 to the same length as the side pieces. Bevel it into a trapezoidal shape by making two rip cuts at 45 degrees, one along each side of the piece. Then, using a side piece as a gauge to make cuts on the spine, cut the rabbet and dadoes across the wide face of the spine to match the side pieces.

The top of the case is a shelf that sits in rabbets cut into the sides and spine. Cut the shelves and top from ¾-inch plywood to the dimensions shown. To cover the plywood edges, attach a strip of ¼×¾-inch hardwood banding to the front edge of each shelf. If you use iron-on edging, the dimensions of the shelves will have to be larger.

GENERAL ASSEMBLY: Assemble the main framework with the case face down. Do a dry run before actually gluing it. Fit one side piece to the edges of the top and shelves. Apply glue to each dado and fit the side and shelves together, making sure the edge of the shelves and the side piece are flush at the front. Secure the joints with 6d finish nails. Set the other side piece and the spine in place. With the case still face down, square it up by measuring corner to corner. Make sure it is not twisted, then let the glued joints set.

Add the back panels while the case is still face down. Each panel should extend from the notch at the back of the side panel to the back edge of the spine. Apply glue to the sides and spine, insert the back pieces, and nail with ⅝-inch brads.

Set the case upright and measure the front. Cut all the pieces for the face frame from 1×2 and 1×6 solid stock.

OPTIONAL EQUIPMENT: The illustration shows the frame around the perimeter of the case, but you may wish to add a center stile, as well as one or more intermediary rails. This would allow you to attach several smaller door panels rather one or two large doors. Join the corners of the face frame together. Nail the frame to the front of the case. Set the nail heads and fill holes and gaps with wood putty. Then sand and apply the finish of your choice.

Item	Material	Size	Qty
Sides	¾" plywood	5½×72"	2
Back panels	¼" plywood	21½×72"	2
Top	¾" plywood		1
Shelves	¾" plywood		5
Face frame top	1×6 pine	29"	1
Face frame sides	1×2 pine	72"	2
Face frame bottom	1×6 pine	29"	1
Spine	2×4 pine	72"	1
Trim	Hardwood	¼×¾"×8'	

MATERIALS LIST

6d finish nails; ⅝" brads; white carpenter's glue; wood putty; paint, stain, or varnish

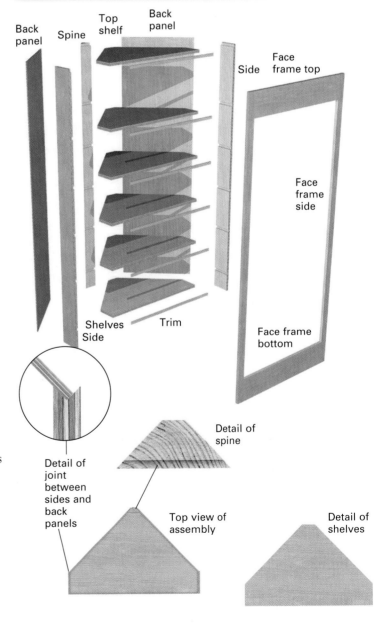

Back panel · Spine · Top shelf · Back panel · Side · Face frame top · Face frame side · Face frame bottom · Shelves · Side · Trim · Detail of joint between sides and back panels · Detail of spine · Top view of assembly · Detail of shelves

HOME OFFICES

Technological innovations make home offices more productive all the time. Whether your at-home work space bristles with high-tech gear or simply offers a quiet place to answer mail, it presents a distinct storage challenge.

■ If you use an office only for keeping track of bills and personal records, you can think small: a simple desk or table with drawers.

■ At the next level, you may bring work home occasionally and need a well-organized space where you can attend to it. Or you may need room for a computer and accessories for personal, business, or school use.

■ At the extreme, a growing number of people have home-based businesses, which may require a full-blown office space.

THE PERSONAL TOUCH

If your office needs are only of a personal nature, you may find sufficient space in a corner of a bedroom or the kitchen.

■ A SMALL FIREPROOF STORAGE BOX or safe is a good investment for storing important documents. These boxes provide safekeeping as well as out-of-sight storage.

■ TWO-DRAWER FILING CABINETS take up little room, but they swallow up reams of paper and pounds of would-be clutter.

■ CARDBOARD BANKERS' BOXES, wide enough for file folders, are handy for storing records you don't need to retrieve often.

Any of these containers will help you organize bills, legal documents, health and tax records, insurance papers, and warranties.

A tackle box or drawer organizer will give you an orderly place for pens, pencils, paper, and other office supplies. It sure beats digging through a disorderly drawer stuffed with random tools and scraps.

Finding space for a computer is tougher. A dining room or other quiet, central space often works well if the computer is to be used by adults for records, by children for school work, and by everyone for entertainment.

Home offices don't have to be separate rooms. A corner can get the job done, as in this family room. Built-in furniture works well in these instances, and you can design the storage spaces to fit your needs.

STRICTLY BUSINESS

While the idea of working at home may be appealing, it can be difficult to execute. A successful business office at home requires careful planning. It should be somewhat secluded for privacy, should have ample, uncluttered surfaces for equipment, and must have storage space for files, supplies, books, catalogs, and anything else relevant to your business. Here are some things to consider when locating and organizing a home-based business office:

■ Unless you expect to have frequent clients visiting your office, your space need not look elaborate. In fact, many people find they work best in spartan surroundings.

■ Even if your office is simple, pay attention to details. Check the natural lighting from windows. If it's not sufficient, plan to add some. Make sure you have enough electrical outlets and telephone jacks to handle the equipment you require—a separate telephone line, computer and printer, fax machine, calculator, and perhaps a personal copy machine.

■ Office machines require plenty of space. Plan plenty of desktop or countertop room for a computer, printer, fax machine, telephone, and copier.

■ Protect sensitive equipment from environmental hazards: dust, pets, coffee or soda spills. Dust covers are a good investment. Office furniture that closes up and hides equipment while not in use is good, but make sure when the desk units roll out or open up that the machines have space to "breathe" so they don't overheat.

■ Zone storage space around your desk according to how often you use the items. Find space in a primary zone—within 24 to 30 inches of your desktop—for items you use frequently, such as pens, notepads, a dictionary or other reference books, the telephone, or file folders for current projects. Items that you don't use every day should be allocated to shelf or drawer space a medium distance from your work surface. Last, find a place for things you use rarely, such as permanent files, records, and only occasionally used reference books.

■ Use space above and below your work surface efficiently. Build shelves above the desk for zone-one items. Lateral files below or alongside your desk take up less space than

traditional three- or four-drawer file cabinets. Shelves or files on an adjacent wall are fine for zone-two and -three items.

■ Take advantage of the many commercial accessories to keep clutter off your desktop. Many of these storage devices are designed to mount on walls or the side of desks.

Many desks are designed with the home office in mind. This one hides away the computer's printer when it isn't in use.

This office storage is set up perfectly. The primary zone is the desktop. Drawers serve as secondary storage. And the wall bookcase holds reference books used only occasionally.

HOME OFFICES
continued

CONSTRUCTING A DESKTOP COMPUTER CENTER

This easy-to-build desktop computer center saves space and organizes your computer and its ever-increasing number of accessories.

With today's advancing technology, you probably will upgrade your computer, fax, and printer every few years. So it makes little sense to build a shelf system designed to fit precisely the machines you now own. A simple desk with open shelves is usually best. This desktop unit is designed to sit on top of a pair of two-drawer file cabinets so it can be moved easily or rearranged with changes in equipment. Or you can mount it between taller pieces of office furniture, such as a shelf system or a three- or four-drawer file cabinet. Make the desk between 24 and 36 inches deep (here it's 30 inches), and be sure to attach it to units sufficiently deep and strong enough to support it.

STYLE AND STRENGTH: The desktop is made out of a double layer of ¾-inch cabinet-grade birch plywood to provide a strong base for the equipment and a smooth writing surface that won't warp. The two 20-inch side supports keep the top from sliding off the file cabinets. Attach them to the bottom piece of plywood before gluing the two pieces together. Cut the plywood to size, and attach the side supports to the good face of the bottom piece with flat-headed screws driven through the rougher side. Place the good side of the second piece of plywood face

Item	Material	Dimensions	Qty
Desktop	¾" plywood	29¼×58½"	2
Shelf	¾" plywood	14½×59¼"	1
Front trim	1×2 birch	60"	1
Back trim	1×2 birch	60"	1
Side trim	1×2 birch	30"	2
Shelf trim	1×1 birch	60"	1
Shelf supports	1×6 birch	16"	3
Supports	1×4 birch	20"	2

MATERIALS LIST

1¼" #6 oval headed screws; 1¼" #6 roundhead screws; 6d finish nails; pull-out keyboard shelf unit; white carpenter's glue; wood putty; paint, stain, or varnish as needed

down. Apply squiggles of carpenter's glue and place the piece with the side supports on top of the first, with the supports facing upward. Drive in 1¼-inch ovalhead screws around the perimeter to tie the pieces together. Take care not to drive the heads below the surface or they may poke through the finished side. Miter the 1×2 solid birch trim and attach it to the edges of the desktop with glue and 6d finish nails.

The shelf that holds the monitor and printer can be constructed of the same birch plywood. Attach 1×1 trim to the front and back edges of the shelf with glue and 6d finish nails. Use 1×6 or larger solid birch for the supports. The width of the supports depends on how much you want to store under the shelf and how high you want the monitor to be off the desktop. Cut ⅜-inch rabbets into the top edges of the end supports. These will strengthen the joint and eliminate the need to apply trim to the ends.

CUBICLES: If you like little storage cubicles, you can add center supports to further divide the space below the shelf.

The shelf is designed simply to sit on top of the desktop. If you're concerned that it might get bumped off, attach it to the desktop with angle brackets at the rear of each support.

Fill all nail holes and other defects in the plywood, sand the pieces smooth, and finish to your preference. Place the desktop on file cabinets, then mount the slide-out keyboard tray where it works best for your typing style. Trays in many different styles are available at office supply or computer retailers.

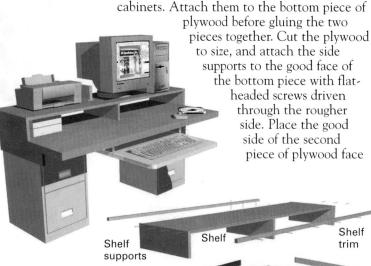

Shelf supports

Shelf

Shelf trim

Back trim

Desktop

Side trim

Front trim

Support

WORKSHOPS AND HOBBY CENTERS

The living areas in your home are not confined to the living, family, or dining rooms. We spend much of our free time on hobbies, such as crafts, woodworking, sewing, painting or other arts, or rebuilding that favorite '48 coupe.

While these activities have particular storage requirements suited to each, there are a lot of commonalities. Here are some things to keep in mind while organizing hobby rooms and associated storage.

■ If you don't have a separate room to devote to hobby space, look for space in the spare bedroom, basement, attic, or garage.

■ If you don't have a large space to devote to a hobby area, don't give up. Many times you can use a corner with great effectiveness. Make use of mobile storage units that you can roll out when you want to pursue your interests—a table on wheels can serve as a craft bench, a sewing table, or even a workbench in the shop.

■ Most hobbies require good lighting. Make sure the room or spot you choose is well lit; try to use natural light effectively.

■ Develop your storage plans to make it easy to put things away. A Phillips-head screwdriver or that spool of light blue thread is not useful if you can't find it the next time you need it.

■ Make sure you have ample surface area to spread out projects on which you're working.

■ Make sure there are enough electrical outlets and that the circuits can carry the amperage load of all equipment you might plug in and have running at the same time.

■ If your craft requires water, locate the activity in a room that has existing plumbing into which you can tie a new sink.

■ Use enclosed storage spaces to protect valuable tools, to keep fabrics clean and dry, or to keep Muffy out of your yarn.

■ Organize tools or supplies in relation to each other, blades with saws, nuts with bolts, needles with thread.

■ Use pullout bins or compartmentalized drawer storage cabinets to sort and store such small items as nuts and bolts or beads and other craft supplies.

■ Think safety. Store hazardous materials or dangerous power tools where children or pets cannot get to them.

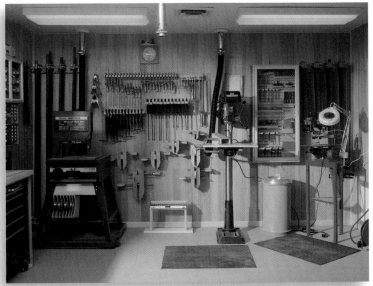

When there's a place for everything, tools are easy to put away— and to find the next time you need them. This woodworker's shop allows the owner to focus on woodwork, not on hunting for tools.

Kitchen cabinetry makes a hobbyist's craft area look like a professional's workshop. Cabinets pack all the essentials: storage, work surface, and lighting. When using cabinets, be sure to design the countertop surface at the correct height for the work you'll be doing.

WORKSHOPS AND HOBBY CENTERS
continued

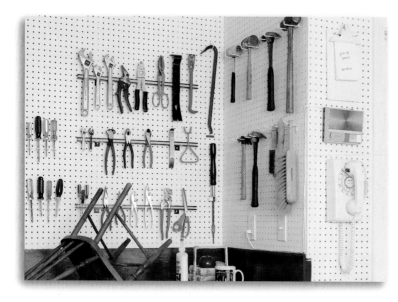

A large, smooth work surface in your shop or hobby center is a must. Being able to find tools and supplies when you need them is also important.

Fortunately, hundreds of ready-made items are on the market to help keep you organized. Look for these items at specialty storage stores, home centers, lumberyards, and department stores. Here are just a few ideas:

PERFORATED HARDBOARD: You probably associate perforated hardboard (also known as Pegboard) hanging systems with workshops. They're great for organizing tools so they are readily available and easy to put back. But there are so many styles of hooks and hangers now available that you can use these systems in other areas of your home: in the garage for lawn and garden tools, in the rec room for sports equipment, or in your sewing center for spools of thread, scissors, and other supplies.

DRAWER CABINETS: These also were originally designed to hold hardware in the workshop. But they are handy for sewing and craft centers, too. Cabinets are available with small-, medium-, and large-size drawers.

BINS AND BASKETS: Plastic or plastic-coated metal wire bins and baskets are ideal for storing large or bulky supplies for craft and shop projects. Many are stackable to save space; others come in upright units in which the baskets slide out on rails.

PLASTIC BOXES: If you have items that need protection from dust or other environmental conditions, seal them in plastic boxes. These containers come in a multitude of sizes and are clear plastic so you can see their contents. Many are stackable.

CABINETS AND FILES: You can adapt standard kitchen cabinets to meet you needs. In your sewing center, install a pullout towel rack in a standard base cabinet for a convenient place to hang fabrics. Flat file drawer systems are good in a studio or child's room to store large matte boards.

If you use bins, baskets, or drawer cabinets to store items, be sure to develop a labeling system so you know what's in each compartment.

SHELVES: Build shelves above your work areas to store supplies or stackable boxes. In the shop, you'll want to suspend a shelf from the ceiling to store lumber for future projects.

BUILDING A WORKBENCH

Every workshop requires some kind of workbench. If you don't have room for an extensive shop, your bench can be as simple as a flush panel door placed across a set of sawhorses; they can go back in a corner when you've finished a project. At the other extreme, you can purchase complex benches designed for professional woodwork. Here's a bench that falls in between.

You easily can make this bench in a day, and you can make it as complex as you want. Use the dimensions given here or adapt them to your needs. Benches generally range from 6 to 8 feet long and 24 to 36 inches deep. The height of the benchtop should be 30 to 40 inches, whatever is a comfortable working level for you.

Assembling this bench is a matter of cutting stock materials and screwing or nailing them together. In this design, the rear legs extend 3 feet above the bench to serve as a framework on which to mount perforated hardboard, so you can store your tools right in front of you. Connect all the leg supports with 2½-inch lag screws for added support. Also, if you make the bench more than 6 feet wide, use 4×4s instead of 2×4s for the legs.

Make the top out of a double layer of ¾-inch plywood, covered with ¼-inch tempered hardboard. The plywood makes a stable surface that won't warp and the hardboard provides a smooth surface you can replace when it wears out. If you want to make the bench fancier,

you can build a cabinet or drawer unit into the area under the bench. Then you would have enclosed storage for expensive or delicate tools. A locking cabinet would protect your treasured tools from your curious kids and mooching neighbor.

MATERIALS LIST

Item	Material	Size	Qty
Rear legs	2×4 pine	72"	2
Front legs	2×4 pine	33"	2
Top front brace	2×4 pine	72"	1
Top back brace	2×4 pine	69"	1
Top side braces	2×4 pine	28½"	2
Bottom long braces	2×4 pine	66"	2
Bottom short braces	2×4 pine	25½"	2
Bottom shelf	½" plywood	25½×69"	1
Lower back	½" plywood	22½×69"	1
Top, base	¾" plywood	30×72"	2
Top, surface	¼" hardboard	30×72"	1
Top brace	2×2 pine	62"	1
Back support	2×2 pine	39"	1
Tool board	⅛" perforated hardboard	36×73½"	1
Top trim	1×3 hardwood	73½"	1
Top trim	1×3 hardwood	30¾"	2

2½" lag screws; 3d and 6d finish nails; white carpenter's glue

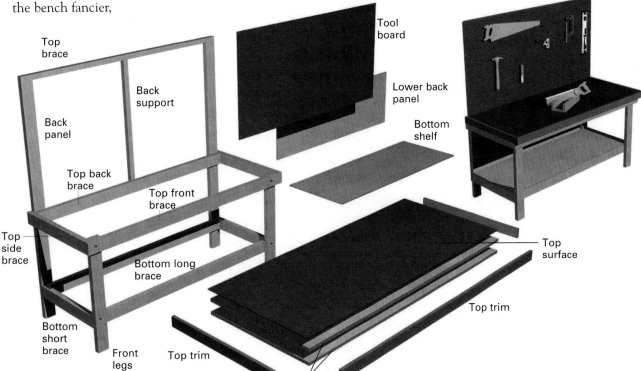

Top brace

Back support

Back panel

Top back brace

Top front brace

Top side brace

Bottom long brace

Bottom short brace

Front legs

Top trim

Top base

Tool board

Lower back panel

Bottom shelf

Top surface

Top trim

WORKSHOPS AND HOBBY CENTERS
continued

BUILDING A FOLD-DOWN SEWING TABLE

Storing your sewing machine in its own convenient center will make using it more pleasurable. This sewing center not only puts the machine at your fingertips, it also provides a handy work surface.

The heart of this project is the fold-down sewing machine shelf. The materials list and drawing show everything you need if you're going to build the entire cabinet. Or you can build the fold-down sewing shelf into an existing bookcase.

Most sewing machines require a space 9 to 10 inches deep, so a common 12-inch-deep bookcase would be an ideal home for the sewing shelf. The plans here are for a 3-foot-wide unit, which is also a common bookcase size. Another option: Build the unit into a spare closet for a true hideaway system.

If you're starting from scratch, build the cabinet as you would any bookcase (*see page 18*), using the dimensions in the material list. Use rabbet joints at the corners and install the one fixed shelf (the highest one) by cutting dadoes into the sides of the cabinet.

The fold-down work surface opens to reveal the sewing machine in its stored position on a fixed shelf. Other supplies can be stored in cabinets under and above the work surface.

Before installing the sewing table, determine the most comfortable working height—usually between 26 and 28 inches from the floor. Test the height with your machine placed on a trial surface. Make the table wide enough to hold your machine comfortably; here we use 30 inches.

The flat, fold-down work surface can be marked with a grid that is convenient for layout and pattern work. Using this design requires that you lift the sewing machine from its storage shelf onto the fold-down work area when you want to use it, then lift it back to its storage area when you're done.

EASY ALTERNATIVE

Incorporating a movable tray will allow you to glide the machine out to its work position. The tray rolls along grooves routed into the surface of the shelf and the worktable. It eliminates the lifting, but this system has a small drawback: The tabletop then is not a smooth workplace. But if you use the machine frequently and have to put it away after each session, the added convenience may make routing the grooves and doing the extra construction worthwhile.

Make the rolling tray from ¾-inch plywood cut slightly larger than the base of your sewing machine. Purchase four small wheels and attach them to the sides of the tray so they project down below the bottom of the tray. Attach the wheels with screws.

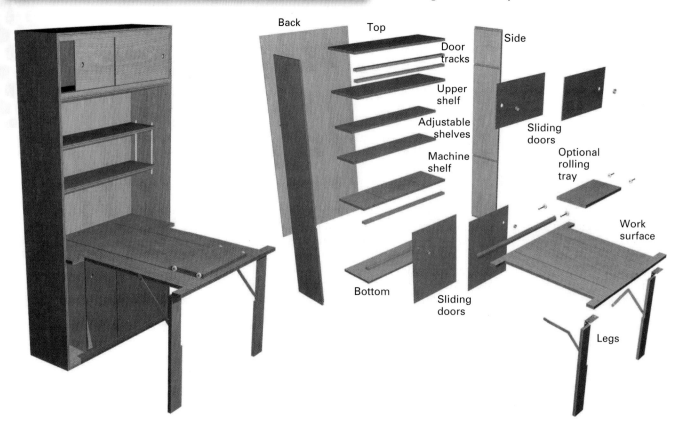

MATERIALS LIST

Item	Material	Dimensions	Qty
Sides	¾" plywood	12×68¾"	2
Top	¾" plywood	12×35"	1
Bottom	¾" plywood	12×35"	1
Back	¼" plywood	35¼×77¼"	1
Upper shelf	¾" plywood	12×35"	1
Machine shelf	¾" plywood	11¾×35"	1
Adj. shelves	¾" plywood	8×35"	2
Work surface	¾" plywood	34¾×30	1
Legs	¾" plywood	3½×26"	2
Movable tray	¾" plywood	8¥16"	1
Door tracks	oak	¾×1½×34½"	4
Sliding doors	¼" plywood	18×10"	2
Sliding doors	¼" plywood	18×22"	2

screws and nails as needed; four casters; one 1½×34" brass piano hinge; two 1½×3½ butt hinges; two locking folding braces; three latches; veneer tape; white carpenter's glue; wood putty; paint, stain, or varnish as needed

PLYWOOD BASE: Measure the width and height of the bay that will house the sewing table, then subtract ⅛ inch from the width and ¼ inch from the height. Using these dimensions, cut the table from ¾-inch cabinet-grade plywood that matches the material from which the case is made.

Cut 3½-inch-wide cutouts to accommodate the legs. The length of these cutouts depends on the length of the legs, which depends on the height you have calculated for the work surface. Using the same ¾-inch plywood, or matching 1×4 solid wood stock, make the legs to fit in the notches.

Cut a piece of cabinet-grade plywood for the storage shelf inside the cabinet. Cut the plywood ¾ inch narrower than the width of the case because, when folded up, the worktable lies flush with the front face of the case. Note also that any shelves above the storage shelf that will be covered by the worktable when it is folded up should be ¾ inch narrower than the case.

If you intend to install the rolling tray, now is the time to lay out and rout ⅛-inch (or the width of the wheels) grooves in both the table and the storage shelf. Also cut ¾-inch dado grooves in the sides of the cabinet at the height of the storage shelf.

ASSEMBLY: Before assembly, check that pieces fit, then sand and finish them to match the cabinet. Fasten the legs to the worktable

using a pair of 3½-inch butt hinges. Install the storage shelf in the cabinet, gluing and nailing it in the dadoes.

Attach the fold-up worktable to the storage shelf by screwing one flange of a piano hinge, cut to the full length of the shelf, to the back edge of the worktable, then to the front edge of the shelf.

With the table flat, position the legs vertically. Hold an open, locking brace at a 45-degree angle to mark the screw locations on the edges of the table and legs. Drill pilot holes and install the braces. For a more finished appearance, mark the position of the locking braces with the legs folded up, then remove the legs and braces and rout a mortise channel in the edge of each leg for the brace. Then reinstall the braces.

Apply veneer tape to all the exposed plywood edges. Sand and finish to match the rest of the unit. Install barrel-bolt or other more attractive latches of your choice to secure each leg and the worktable in place when it is in the up position.

ADDING SHELVES AND DOORS:

If you've installed the fold-down table in a premade cabinet with adjustable shelves, you may have to rip a portion off the shelves above the fold-down worktable so it will close in a flush position.

If you are building your own cabinet, plan ahead by using adjustable shelf supports on the sides of the cabinet (or drill a series of evenly spaced holes for shelf pins) so the shelves will be movable.

You easily can add doors to the shelf sections at the top and bottom of the cabinet (*see illustration*). You can also attach prefabricated sliding door track to the front of the shelf edges. Then cut doors from ¼-inch plywood that matches the rest of the unit. The bottom prefabricated track should be shallow, ⅛–³⁄₁₆ inch. The top track should be deep enough to allow clearance for the door panels to be lifted into place. Prefabricated tracks are available in wood, plastic, and metal versions. In this case, however, the tracks stick above the wood surface and may catch items that you move in and out of the shelves.

Alternatively, you can rout grooves into the shelves before you install them in the book case. This requires a little more woodworking skill to make sure the grooves align in the lower and upper shelves. Cut doors out of the same ¾-inch cabinet-grade plywood stock, finish them to match the unit, and install them with your choice of hinges.

Most basements, attics, and garages could echo comedian Rodney Dangerfield's famous double-negative lament, "I don't get no respect." They're often casual catch-alls instead of orderly storage areas. Stuff piles up too quickly. But once you dig to the bottom of it, you'll be amazed at the space available. The trick is to use it thoughtfully. Look at the examples below, then study the opportunities in this chapter to reshape your catch-all areas, respectfully.

ATTIC, BASEMENT, GARAGE, AND YARD SOLUTIONS

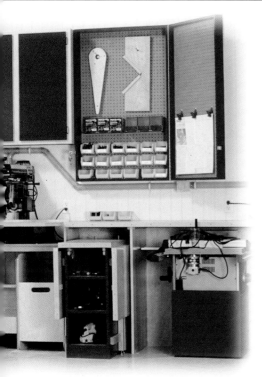

They may not look like luxuries, but attics, basements, and garages hide a wealth of storage potential. And don't forget the great outdoors; a shed can stash loads of gear, taking pressure off other areas.

Unfinished attics or basements are logical places to store seasonal items— holiday decorations, clothes, and other things you use only occasionally—or items you've put into long-term storage, such as a wedding gown or baby items. These areas, along with the garage, usually become the collecting places for bulky items: bicycles and other sports equipment, patio furniture, grills, camping gear, lawn tools.... The list goes on, and the space fills up.

Organization will make the space more comfortable and efficient. The major goals are to increase storage capacity and to improve access to stored possessions.

Out-of-the-way places in attics, basements, and garages often are unfinished and thus can house storage systems built of inexpensive, unfinished materials. These are ideal areas in which to experiment with woodworking projects and to perfect do-it-yourself skills. Many projects on the following pages are simple enough for the beginner or can inspire more complex projects for those with advanced carpentry skills. Lumber, plywood, and fasteners are the usual construction materials. If you have a circular saw, radial-arm saw, or tablesaw, you can cut the pieces yourself. If not, many home centers or lumberyards will do the heavy-duty cutting for you.

IN THIS SECTION

Unfinished Attic Solutions
80

Finished Attic
Solutions **82**

Basement Solutions **84**

Building Adjustable Utility
Shelves **86**

Building a Wine Rack **87**

Attacking Garage Gridlock
88

Climbing the Walls **90**

Buying Solutions **91**

Storage Solutions in Your
Yard **92**

Building a Storage
Shed **93**

UNFINISHED ATTIC SOLUTIONS

Many attics are not usable for storage because they are too small or too congested by insulation, ductwork, plumbing, or roof framing. But steep roofs supported by rafters rather than trusses usually cover some useful storage space.

In thinking about attic storage, space is only the first consideration. You also need adequate access, flooring, and light. Also, most attics are not heated or air-conditioned, so be sure the items you plan to store there can withstand the environment.

GAINING ACCESS

The simplest form of attic access is through a push-up hatch, or scuttle, often located in a hallway or closet. Many of these hatches are small, with just enough room for a person to clamber through for maintenance. In these cases, the attic probably wasn't meant for storage. You'll need an opening at least 30 inches square for any serious storage utility.

Getting items up through the opening is a concern. You *could* haul out the step ladder each time and risk breaking your neck as you heft boxes up the ladder and heave them through the hatch. A fixed ladder, mounted on an adjacent wall, offers a sturdier solution. Better yet, fold-down stairs provide handy, easy-to-hide access. Prefabricated units are available at home centers, and installation is not difficult. These stairs don't waste floor space, they're invisible when not in use, and good ones are more stable and comfortable than ladders.

A fixed stairway offers far more convenience and stability, but space for permanent stairs is even harder to find than storage. And stairway construction is best left to professionals.

ORGANIZING THE UNFINISHED ATTIC

To maximize storage space in an attic, you must use odd-shaped areas, sharp angles, and limited headroom to the best advantage. In most cases, it isn't a problem but rather an opportunity to develop ingenious solutions. Generally, an attic has three areas with storage potential: along the sloping walls, against gable ends, and right in the center under the ridge beam. To take advantage of those areas, try these ideas:
■ Make sure there is maximum floor space. If floor joists are exposed, cover them with plywood or other flooring. Be careful when

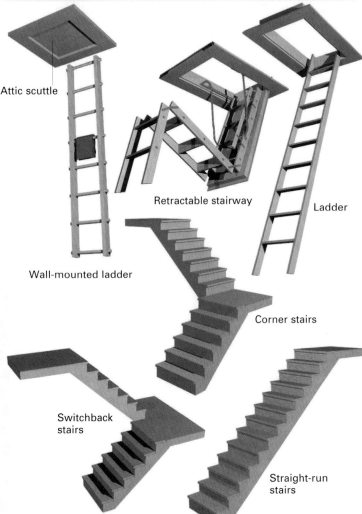

Attic scuttle

Retractable stairway

Ladder

Wall-mounted ladder

Corner stairs

Switchback stairs

Straight-run stairs

applying flooring that you do not compress insulation, which reduces its effectiveness.

■ If you live in an area with temperature extremes, consider insulating the roof so the space is not blistering hot in the summer and ice cold in the winter.

■ Install vents in the roof, gable, or soffit to keep air moving in the attic.

■ Store items off the floor, away from dirt, bugs, and moisture. Discarded shipping pallets are handy if they will fit through your attic access. The attic is the perfect place for old shelving. Garage sales, flea markets, and thrift shops are good sources. Look for units that come apart if you have limited access.

■ Don't store items in rows more than two deep.

■ Leave pathways so you can reach everything. The last thing you want is an impenetrable wall of belongings that requires unstacking and stacking in tight quarters.

■ Stackable plastic containers seal out dirt, dust, and bugs. If you use cardboard boxes, seal them with tape and mark them so you won't have to open rows of boxes to find something.

■ If you store seasonal hanging clothes, protect them with plastic zip-up garment bags. Cardboard garment boxes sold by moving companies are not as bug proof but will keep dust off your clothes.

Four 2×4s, some 1×3 cleats, and three pieces of ¾-inch plywood (*right*) or just the plywood and some chain and hardware (*bottom center*) are all it takes to make some handy shelves in the space below attic rafters. If you hang the shelves with chains, you can attach them in one of three ways:

■ Insert screws with washers through the chain links.

■ Drill holes through the shelves, slip the chain through the holes, then run a bolt through a chain link.

■ Or simply tie a sturdy rope between the chain links and rest the shelf on the rope.

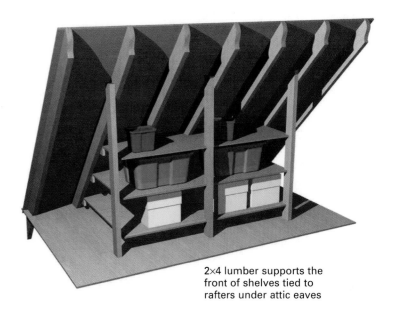

2×4 lumber supports the front of shelves tied to rafters under attic eaves

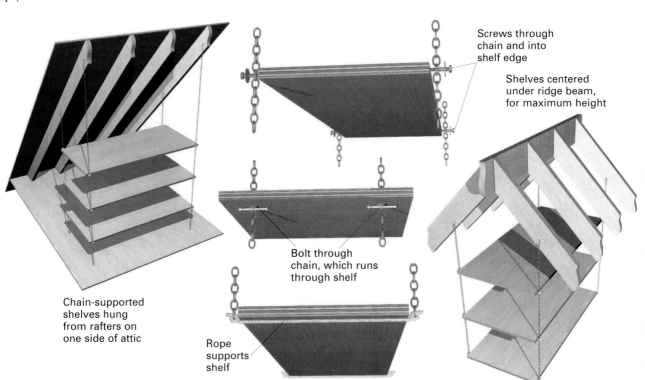

Screws through chain and into shelf edge

Shelves centered under ridge beam, for maximum height

Bolt through chain, which runs through shelf

Chain-supported shelves hung from rafters on one side of attic

Rope supports shelf

FINISHED ATTIC SOLUTIONS

*In remodeling this attic, the homeowners took advantage of the storage potential along a knee wall, **right**, and gable end, **below**. Cabinets and bookshelves fit well in both areas.*

A large unfinished attic can be developed as usable living space— an extra bedroom, an office, or a child's play room. As you plan, think about potential storage spaces. Because of the many odd angles in attics, it's a lot easier to build storage units as you remodel the attic, rather than after the fact.

You'll want to take advantage of the floor space in the center of the room for living space, so concentrate storage space along the outside walls and gable ends. Many times these areas become wasted space. For example, it's easy to nail up some 2×4s and drywall to create vertical knee walls. But in doing so, you've lost that potential storage space in the eaves behind the knee wall. If you plan ahead, you could build finished, recessed shelves or drawer units into these under-utilized spaces.

An alternative to building knee walls is to finish the inside of the roof right down to the attic floor, then install standard cabinetry in the eaves, essentially creating a knee wall

with the cabinets. You'll lose some of the countertop depth on top of the cabinets because of the slanted roofline, but it will be deep enough to serve as a shelf.

Gable ends in attic and half-stories also harbor prime storage space. These are ideal areas for shelving, entertainment centers, or standard kitchen cabinets.

A large dormer is big enough to create a walk-in closet if you are remodeling the main space as a bedroom. A small dormer usually contains enough space for a built-in desk, creating a small office with good natural light.

You may decide to finish only a portion of the attic, leaving the remainder for storage. In this case, install a door between the two areas so you have easy access to the unfinished portion. If this access is in a knee wall, you may have to cut down a door. Walled-off, unfinished areas also present opportunities for children's secret play rooms, where they can also store toys. If you do this, be safety conscious. Don't leave the area in a bare-bones mode; sheath or drywall the rafters and studs and make sure the flooring is secure.

Attics make great offices if customers and clients rarely visit. An attic location has a sense of separation so work is conveniently accessible—yet readily escapable.

BUILDING AN UNDER-THE-EAVES CLOSET

A good way to take advantage of under-the-eaves space when remodeling an attic is to build a closet. The necessary materials for this project vary with each job, depending on the closet's size, shape, and the slope of the roofline. Whatever space you have to work with, make the front of the closet as tall as you can.

Start by insulating the spaces between the rafters. Frame the closet with 2×4 studs, then finish the inside of the roof and closet walls with drywall or paneling to match the rest of the room. You can use drywall or paneling inside the closet, too, or line it with aromatic cedar (*see page 53*).

To divide the space into useful cubicles, you could use any of the closet organizing systems outlined earlier in the Bedrooms and Closets section (*pages 44–57*).

BASEMENT SOLUTIONS

A walkout basement offers the advantage of plentiful daylight. This one also benefits from a solid wall of storage. The bottom tier of cabinets can hold games and toys. Upper shelves showcase books.

Just as a kitchen service bar hides countertop clutter from diners, a counter-topped half-wall shields this desk from a basement family room.

When it comes to heavy-duty storage space, a basement is a natural. It's a big concrete vault, often unfinished, generally out of sight; there's no load limit to weight, as there is on a joist-supported floor; and gravity works in your favor: A basement is easier to fill than to unload.

Too often, however, an unfinished basement becomes a repository for large items: boxes of seasonal decorations and clothing, sports gear, or anything that gets in the way upstairs or outside. As with any other space in your home, tapping the potential of the basement means getting organized.

Utilities and moisture are two hurdles you must cross in the basement. Dealing with the first is a matter of organization. A wet basement may be harder to overcome.

Even before you moved in, your basement already was the home of the furnace, water heater, and water conditioner and probably was plumbed and wired for laundry facilities. While furnace fires, bursting water heaters, and overflowing washing machines are rare, they do happen. Don't tinker with disaster. Keep stored items away from these units, either by walling off the areas or by designating them off-limits to storage.

Deal with any major moisture problems before using a basement for storage. If water leaks more than occasionally, call in an expert. The most extreme remedy is to excavate around the exterior, install drain tile, and reseal the foundation from the outside. It may be possible, however, to solve the problem by installing a sump pump.

Minor condensation problems and excess humidity, common to most basements in the summer, can be reduced by scrubbing the walls and floor to remove mildew, painting them with a waterproofing compound, then using a dehumidifier to keep the moisture level low.

Even if you correct these problems or have a dry basement, store items off the floor. Concrete tends to wick water and transfer it to flat permeable material that is in contact with it for extended periods. Cardboard boxes, for example, should never be stored directly on a concrete floor.

The projects shown here will help keep items off the floor to prevent damage. Just as with attics, if you plan to completely remodel an unfinished basement, work your storage strategies into the overall remodeling plan. If you're going to convert the space into a recreation room, office, or bedroom, consider leaving one area unfinished to serve as your heavy-duty storage headquarters.

USING SPACE UNDER STAIRWAYS

Make use of the space under stairs, whether you install simple shelves under unfinished stairs or finish off the space with drywall and built-in shelves. Use this space as a long-term pantry for canned goods, as a locker room for the sports equipment, or as a library of books and games in a finished family room. If the stairway runs down the middle of the basement, rather than against a wall, divide the under-stairs space in half lengthwise so you have storage for different items on each side.

Many basement stairs are L-shaped and provide an opportunity to build two storage areas. Closing in the high end of the stairway creates closet space. Use the space under the low stairs for shelves. When building basement projects, always use pressure-treated lumber (which resists the ravages of moisture) on the floor and against exterior walls. Attach it with masonry nails or lag screws and shields. Other lumber can be common dimension pine, fir, or plywood.

Enclose the space under the stairs completely if you want to keep items out of sight or dust free. Essentially you're building a closet under the stairs, but inside the doors, you can have shelves rather than closet rods. You also can install any of the closet organization systems described in the closet chapter. Divide a long stairway into more than one enclosure.

A variation on the enclosed concept is to build rolling bins out of plywood using basic bookshelf-building techniques. The bins can be simple boxes into which you dump items or to which you can add shelves. These are handy if you use the room for hobbies. Bins with the correct supplies can be rolled right to your work area. Bins with casters also are available commercially.

BUILDING ADJUSTABLE UTILITY SHELVES

Sturdy utility shelves thrive in basements. Like healthy houseplants, they seem to grow fuller in their ideal environment. Buy or build heavy-duty, reinforced shelving if you expect to store boxes of books, files, or other hefty loads.

The shelves in this project get their strength from supports at the front and back. The framework is made of eight 2×4 uprights with adjustable shelving strips and 2×4 front and back rails that hold up interlocking shelf supports.

The plywood shelves can be up to 2 feet deep and 4 feet long. The number of vertical supports depends on the total length and the weight you'll put on the shelves. With two interior uprights, you'll have shelf spans of about 32 inches for an 8-foot long unit. If you use ¾-inch plywood shelves, spans could be 3–4 feet.

Begin by toenailing 14½-inch-long 2×4 blocking between the appropriate ceiling joists where the uprights will intersect the joists. Screw heavy-duty adjustable shelf supports to one side of each upright. Then screw one set of end uprights to the blocking and to the 2×4 soleplate just above the wall (assuming the shelf sits against a wall), making sure the shelf support hardware is facing out and the upright is plumb. Install the other end uprights in the same manner, 8 feet from the first set. The middle uprights should be spaced 31 inches on-center from the other ones. To make the unit more stable, nail pressure-treated 2×4 blocks between the front and back of each pair of uprights at the floor level.

Build the shelves by cutting the rails 28 inches long so they'll fit flush with and between the uprights. You can cut the plywood shelves into 28-inch lengths to match the rails, in which case there will be a 3-inch gap between adjacent shelves. Or you can cut them into 31-inch lengths, which are centered on the rails and notched on the ends so they'll fit around the uprights. Nail or screw the shelves onto the rails. If you expect extremely heavy loads on the shelves, you can add 2×4 supports under the side edges of the shelves. Then attach the matching hardware shelf supports on the outward side of the rails to match the supports on the uprights.

You then can insert the shelves at the height suited to what you are storing. The bottom set of shelves should be 8–12 inches off the floor to ensure good air circulation around stored items.

MATERIALS LIST

Item	Material	Dimensions	Qty
Uprights	2×4 pine	84"	8
Upright supports	2×4 treated pine	21"	4
Rails	2×4 pine	96"	9
Shelves	¾" plywood	24×28 or 31"	9

10d finish nails; 16d common nails; 2" #8 drywall screws; eight heavy shelf standards

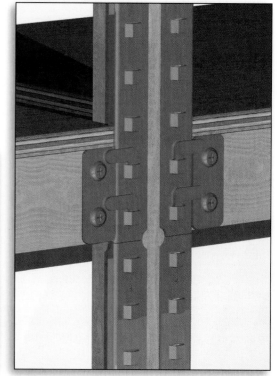

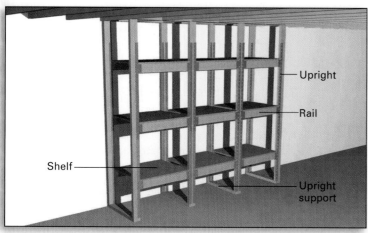

BUILDING A WINE RACK

A cool basement is an ideal place to store wine, which favors a constant temperature of 55–60° F and minimal direct light. You can store wine in a variety of rack styles, but the bottles should be stored on their sides. Standard shelves will work fine or you could use bins or cubicle units set on their sides.

Here's an easy-to-build wine rack that you can make as a portable unit or a cabinet. Or you can expand it in any direction, even floor-to-ceiling if you like. To increase the height or width of the wine rack, change the front and back crosspiece measurements in increments of 2¼ inches and the height of the side panels in 3½-inch increments.

Oak and cherry are beautiful woods for this project, but it may be difficult to find 11¼-inch-wide boards that are not warped. Redwood or stained pine are easier to work with and less expensive. The closet dowels are usually available only in fir, but you can stain them to match a darker wood.

Cut the two end pieces as a single unit from one piece of 1×12. Draw a line through the middle of the board, perpendicular to the long edge. Drill two 1-inch-diameter holes on this line, each 3 inches from either edge. Be sure to clamp a scrap board to the back of the good board while you drill to avoid tearing out the wood when the bit goes through. Draw lines on both sides of the circles to connect them. Cut the board down the centerline, then use a jigsaw to cut along the lines between the two now half-circles. Use a compass or large coin to draw the rounded edges on the top corners, then cut them with the jigsaw. Sand and smooth all the rounded edges.

If you wish to cuts slots for hand grips, as shown, drill two more sets of 1-inch-diameter holes, connect them, and cut them out with the jigsaw.

Cut the eight crosspieces from 1×2 hardwood or rip them from another piece of the 1×12 stock you used for the ends. Take

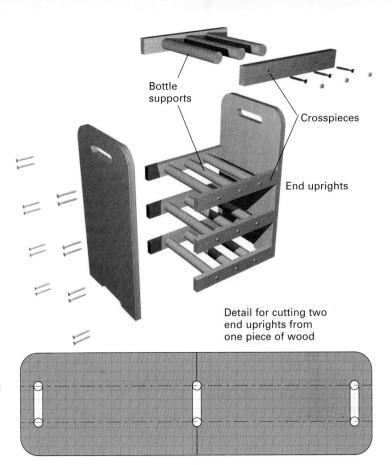

Bottle supports

Crosspieces

End uprights

Detail for cutting two end uprights from one piece of wood

care that these pieces are cut perfectly square and exactly the same length.

The bottom crosspieces should be 1 inch above the bottom of the end pieces. Position each additional crosspiece 3½ inches above the previous one. Use bar clamps to hold the end pieces to the top and bottom crosspieces while you drill pilot poles through the end pieces and into the ends of the crosspieces. Counterbore the holes if you want to conceal the screwheads. Fasten these four crosspieces in place with 2-inch brass or pan-head screws. Position and attach the remaining crosspieces in the same manner.

Cut sections of 1¼-inch dowel stock for the bottle supports, again making sure that the ends are cut perfectly square. Position the supports equally across the crosspieces, drill pilot holes (with counterbores if you want to conceal the screws), and insert screws to hold the supports in place.

To add strength to the rack, cut rectangular mortises in the end pieces for all the crosspieces to fit into and counterbore holes in the crosspieces for the bottle supports.

To conceal the screws, use a plug cutter to make plugs out of the same wood stock or buy precut tapered plugs that match the wood. Glue them into the counterbored holes; when dry, sand them flush with the surface. Sand the entire unit and finish with stain, oil, or varnish (see page 23).

MATERIALS LIST

Item	Material	Length	Qty
End uprights	1×12 hardwood	20"	2
Crosspieces	1×2 hardwood	12¾"	8
Bottle supports	1¼" dowels	9¾"	12

2" #8 brass or pan-head screws; screw plugs (optional); stain, oil, or varnish as needed

ATTACKING GARAGE GRIDLOCK

Whether you create space for a shop or just store lawn and garden tools and furniture, concentrate garage storage around the edges so you still have room for vehicles.

The goal of creating storage space in the garage should be to take advantage of the peripheral spaces without intruding on the parking area.

Does your garage have an open ceiling and a peaked roof, supported by rafters rather than a truss system? If so, the overhead space may be usable for light storage. Does the garage have open floor space not occupied by cars? Shelving systems can go here. What about wall space? It's useful for hanging yard tools, bicycles, and other sports equipment. More important, does your garage have a car in it?

Or, like so many garages, is there so much clutter that your car has been relegated to the driveway or street?

If you have an unheated, unattached garage and you live in a cold climate, avoid storing anything in it that might be damaged by freezing. With an attached garage, you may be able to direct sufficient heat to the garage to prevent freezing problems.

Each garage has its own possibilities. See whether you can adapt some of the ideas on the following pages so you have room for more than your vehicles.

USING SPACE ABOVE THE CAR

LADDER SHELVES: A ladder-style shelf uses space above or beside your car to get items off the floor. If you have a sedan, the shelf can be mounted in the space above the front hood of the car, taking advantage of that wasted space.

Ladder shelves are simple construction projects, built from 2×4s, 1×2s, and either ½- or ¾-inch plywood. The 2×4 uprights can be secured directly to the ceiling joists with lag screws. Attach the 1×2 cleats to the uprights and nail the plywood on the cleats. This technique also is useful building simple freestanding shelves (*see page 86*).

If the joists run the wrong direction or you don't have many joists, as with some older garages, you can lay 2×4s across the top of the joists and bolt the uprights to the other 2×4s rather than the joists.

MINILOFTS: With a traditional gable-roofed garage, you can lay ⅝- or ¾-inch plywood across the ceiling joists to create a storage loft. You need to make sure the present joists can support the weight you intend to have on the loft. Joists should be good quality 2×6s. If they are not, add new ones before taking this approach. New joists should sit on the top plates of the walls; do not attach them directly to the wall studs. If you don't have access to the top plates, secure ledger strips to the wall studs with lag screws and use joist hangers on the ledgers.

If you have a large gable space with solid joists, you could floor the entire space above the joists. You then could add a fold-down stairway (*see page 80*) for access to this garage attic space.

PLATFORM SHELVES: A storage platform uses the loft concept, except it's built up from floor level. Platforms are ideal if you own a sedan. Be sure to build it high and wide enough so the hood of your car will fit under it, which will allow you to make use of the whole garage space.

A platform shelf is built much like a deck on your house. Attach a 2×4 ledger strip across the wall studs. Run 2×4 end joists out to pressure-treated 4×4 corner posts, which are tied together with another 2×4 along their front edge (the rim joist of a deck). You'll want to install additional 2×4 supports (the joists of a deck) between the ledger and rim joist at 24-inch on-center intervals to help support heavier loads. Use ¾-inch plywood for the platform top.

CLIMBING THE WALLS

Most people already take advantage of the space on garage walls. It's a simple task to nail a 1×4 ledger strip to the wall studs and use short lengths of dowels inserted in holes as hangers for yard and garden tools. You also can buy a wide variety of commercial hooks and hangers designed for this purpose. This is a better solution than hammering spikes or nails directly into the wall studs.

But take advantage of the space right above that ledger strip also. It's another simple task

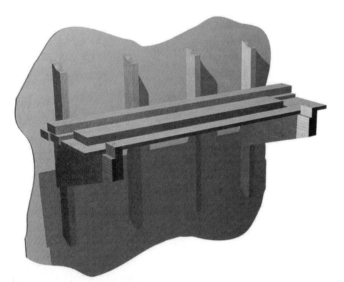

to add some triangular plywood brackets on the ends of the ledger and lay a 12- to 24-inch sheet of plywood across them to serve as a shelf. If you create a long shelf, be sure to add braces in the middle of the shelf also.

Keep these shelves above head height so you can walk around the garage.

You can use these shelves to store related gardening items, such as fertilizer or herbicide containers that should be kept in a high-and-dry location.

This is a good place to install a lumber rack. Depending on the size of lumber you're storing, you could dispense with the plywood shelf and just lay the lumber across the brackets (*left*).

If you have a sufficiently deep or wide garage, consider building a wall storage system (*below*). Use 2×4s to form a floor-to-ceiling framework for a 2-foot-deep case with shelves, then sheath the sides with plywood. Build two identical cases and leave space between them open for lawn equipment or hanging items. You can add to the project by building frame-and-plywood doors and installing them on sliding door tracks mounted across the length of the unit. Build the doors the width of the cases so the space between the cases is open until you slide one or the other door open for access to the shelves in the cases.

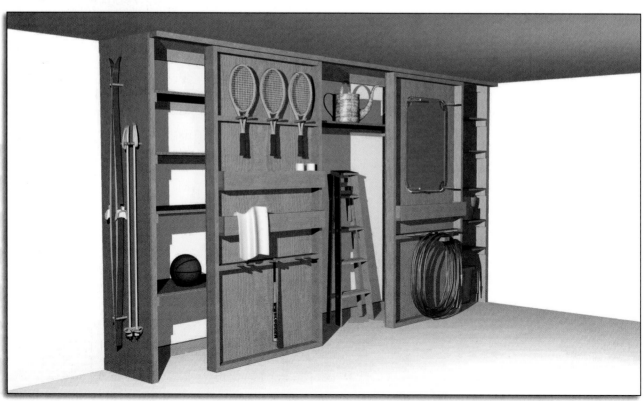

BUYING SOLUTIONS

Many ready-made commercial systems are available now for storing or hanging items in your garage. Some of these also are applicable to basements, attics, or other places in your house. While the systems may take a bit longer to install than nailing a ledger or a shelf to wall studs, their advantage is that most are easy to customize. You can change the configuration and add hangers, shelves, baskets, and bins where and when you need them.

Such systems work best in finished garages. If you have an old garage with exposed stud walls, it's a relatively small job to install drywall, ⅜-inch plywood, or paneling on the walls to create a usable surface. If you use drywall or plywood, you don't have to worry about taping the joints or finishing it if you want a purely utilitarian surface.

Commercial clamps and racks hold hand tools. Power tools get parked in heavy-duty, sliding drawers, safe from dust.

GETTING BICYCLES OFF THE GROUND AND OUT OF THE WAY

Interest in cycling has put cars and bicycles in competition everywhere—on the roadway and in the garage.

Hanging bicycles from the garage wall or ceiling keeps them safe, clean, and out of the way. There are many commercial bike-hanging systems available, ranging from simple vinyl-covered hooks with threaded ends that screw into studs or joists to complex designs that hold your bike as well as helmets and other gear.

You can make a simple homemade rack by hanging two pair of 2×2 uprights to the ceiling joists, adding a brace between them, and attaching 1×4 crosspieces. Cut semicircular notches in each 1×4 to support the bicycle frame. You could create a single unit or a double unit.

STORAGE SOLUTIONS IN YOUR YARD

Don't overlook your yard's potential for storage space. Yard structures can take the pressure off your garage and basement by offering space to store lawn and garden equipment, barbecue grills and accessories, and sports gear. Another benefit of storing such items outside is that you can locate the structures near where the items are used, so you don't have to run to the house or garage when you need something.

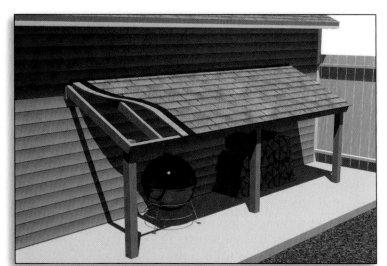

BUILD A LEAN-TO SHED: Whether you make it sophisticated or purely utilitarian, a lean-to shed can store many items—firewood, bicycles, barbecues, garbage cans, or compost bins. You can attach one to the back or side of your garage or house.

It can be as simple as a ledger strip attached to the garage to support the back of a roof with end rafters connected to 4×4 corner posts. Or it can be as complex as an enclosed structure with doors. Use pressure-treated lumber for any outdoor project. Protect the roof of a shed with shingles or use weather-resistant metal or fiberglass roofing panels. Set it on a bed of gravel or a concrete pad.

DEVELOP A GARDENING CENTER: Expand on the lean-to concept to create a gardening or lawn center. To make a useful work space you should do three things: Expand its dimensions, make it weather-tight, and provide a stable foundation.

It's best to set a structure like this on a concrete pad. But you could use a gravel base by setting the outer uprights on concrete footings. For plenty of work room and light, add full-swinging doors. (You could use translucent fiberglass roofing panels, too). Adapt the workbench plans (*see page 75*) by using a slatted top and shelf, and you'll have a great work center that you can locate close to your garden.

MAKE USE OF SPACE UNDER DECKS: If you have a deck more than 4 feet off the ground, take advantage of the space beneath it. This is a good place to store items that can be exposed to weather, such as a barbecue grill or the children's outdoor play items. You can enclose the area beneath the deck by installing lattice or solid paneling around the deck's perimeter if you want to further protect items from the elements. Such covering also helps screen items from view. Remember, you won't have complete protection for items because water will run through the spaces in the decking boards. In cold climates, spaces under decks are ideal for winter storage of your fishing boat or other coverable items.

BUILDING A STORAGE SHED

A storage shed in your yard makes good sense. It may even be a necessity if you don't have a garage or if you have only a small, single-car garage. A simple shed with 2×4 stud walls and rafters is a relatively easy construction project for the above-average do-it-yourselfer. Starting from the ground up is a good way for a beginner to gain experience in carpentry. If you aren't seeking carpentry experience, numerous easy-to-assemble prefabricated shed kits are available on the market.

Prefabricated sheds include traditional wood models, metal units, and high-impact vinyl. The kits come with materials precut and ready to assemble. With basic skills, a tape measure, level, hammer, screwdriver, and a helper, you can erect one in no time. The kits come with detailed instructions specific to the model, so the steps shown here are general in nature to give you an idea of just how easy it is to put a kit shed together.

PREPARE A FOUNDATION AND FLOOR:

Most shed kits do not include floors; they can be purchased as an option, or it's easy to build your own. A solid floor and foundation beneath a shed will prolong its life.

There are two basic options for floors: a concrete slab or a plywood floor constructed on top of 4×4 treated timbers, which in turn rest on a gravel base. In either case, lay out the area with batter boards and mason's lines. Remove the sod from the area, taking about 4 inches around the perimeter of the shed.

If you're going to pour a concrete slab floor, add a 3-inch sand base on the earth. If the shed is extremely large, check with local building codes for foundation and footing requirements. Pour the concrete into 2×4 forms so the top of the slab is 3–4 inches above ground level. You may have to place anchor bolts in the concrete for the shed walls, depending on the manufacturer's instructions.

For a plywood floor, excavate an additional 4 inches and place 4 inches of gravel on the earth. Set three or more (depending on the size of the shed) 4×4 pressure-treated timbers on the gravel, making sure they are level in all directions. Using pressure-treated 2×4s, build a floor frame on top of the timbers with joists spaced 16–24 inches on center, depending on the size of the shed.

Nail ¾-inch pressure-treated plywood on top of the floor frame.

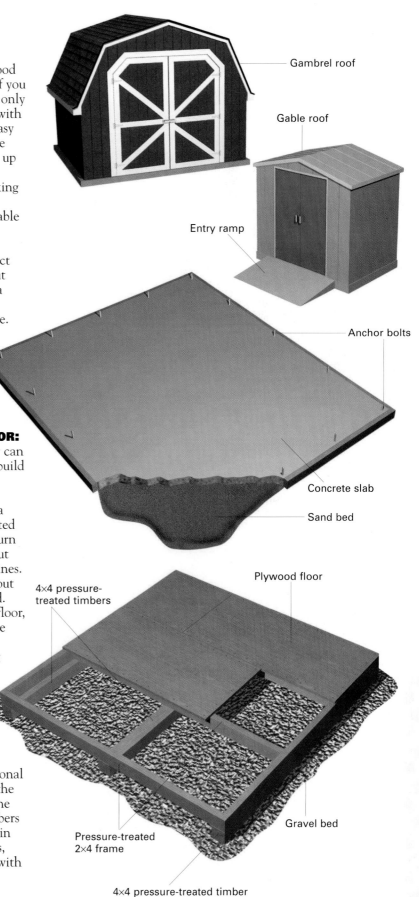

Gambrel roof

Gable roof

Entry ramp

Anchor bolts

Concrete slab

Sand bed

Plywood floor

4×4 pressure-treated timbers

Pressure-treated 2×4 frame

Gravel bed

4×4 pressure-treated timber

BUILDING A STORAGE SHED
continued

Raise the walls: *Raise one of the wall units, nailing it to the plywood floor or bolting it onto the anchor bolts in the concrete. Set it vertical and brace it. Install the adjacent wall in the same manner, then connect the walls according to the manufacturer's instructions. Depending on the style of the shed, you may have to install the gable ends on top of the end walls, or they may be a part of the end walls. If you're building a metal shed, wear gloves to protect yourself from sharp edges.*

Install rafters and roof: *Roof installation varies by manufacturer and style. With a typical gable roof, rafters may come as truss units, or you may have to tie them into a ridge beam that connects the two gables. Install the rafters, then cover the roof with shingles over a plywood sheathing. Or attach metal roofing panels with special sheet-metal roofing screws that have rubber washers to prevent leaks.*

Install doors: *Door styles vary by shed style; you also may have a choice of door type with individual models. Single or double doors can be mounted on hinges to swing open or on tracks to slide open. Some models also have roll-up doors similar to garage doors, but these limit your access to storage space in the gable area of the shed when the door is open. Hinged doors are the easiest to install. With most kits, you simply install the hinges on the door jams and hang the doors.*

Add a ramp: *Whether you use a concrete or a framed plywood floor, the shed will sit 3–6 inches off the ground. This ensures the items in the shed will remain dry. To make access easier, add a ramp in front of the door. Extend the ramp out from the shed 2–3 feet, depending on the slope you want. Use pressure-treated 2×6s, ripped to the appropriate angle and covered with pressure-treated plywood. Set the ramp on a gravel bed so water drains away from the wood.*

GLOSSARY

Actual dimension. Size of boards or lumber, distinguished from "nominal dimensions."

Baseboard. Molding that protects and decorates the joint between a wall and floor.

Bevel. A tool that can be set to specific angles.

Bevel cut. A diagonal cut made through the thickness of a board.

Biscuit. Wooden wafer that bridges and strengthens a joint.

Board. Wood milled with square edges, measuring less than 2 inches thick and more than 3 inches wide.

Brad. A fine finishing nail with a small head.

Bracket. A brace extending from a wall to support a weight, such as a shelf.

Butt joint. Pieces joined by fasteners or adhesives, the joining edges abutting each other rather than overlapping or interlocking.

Butt joint

Carpenter's glue. Yellow and white adhesives formulated specifically for woodworking.

Casing. Trim framing a door, window, or other opening.

Caulk. A puttylike sealant.

Chalk line. A line created by snapping a chalk-covered string against a surface—also to the string itself, which generally is wound into a case filled with powdered chalk.

Circular saw. Power tool with a circular blade that cuts lines faster and straighter than a jigsaw.

Cleat. Lumber used as an anchor or reinforcement.

Clinch. To bend the point of a nail after it has passed through both pieces that it is to fasten, thereby locking them together.

Coped cut. A profile cut on a piece of molding that allows it to be butted tightly against the face of another piece in an inside corner.

Counterbore. To bore a shallow hole into which a screw can be driven and covered by a plug.

Countersink. To drive a nail or screw so its head does not protrude above the surrounding surface.

Cove. A concave form, as in the face of a style of molding.

Crosscut. To saw wood across the pattern of its natural grain.

Dado. A groove cut in one board to form a joint with another.

Dado joint. A joint formed when the end of one member fits into a dado, or groove, cut into another.

Dado joint

Dimension lumber. At least 2 inches thick and 2 inches wide.

Dowels. Wood milled to form rods of various diameters, useful to reinforce joints.

Dowels

Dovetail. A wedge-shape form that slides into a matching notch to form an interlocking joint.

Drywall (also called plaster board) Gypsum panels that cover most new residential interior walls.

Drywall tape. A paper tape applied over drywall joints and finished with a plaster paste.

Ductwork. Piping that conveys heated or cooled air.

Facing. Strips of finely fit and finished wood that cover the front edges of shelves and cabinet frames.

Filler. Pastelike compound used to level indentations in a surface.

Finish. Paint, stain, varnish or any solution that protects a surface.

Flush. On the same plane as or level with an adjoining surface.

Glaze. Paint that is translucent because it has been mixed with water (for latex paint) or glazing liquid (for oil-based paint).

Jigsaw (or saber saw). Maneuverable power saw with a thin saberlike blade.

Kerf. The void created by the width of a saw blade as it cuts.

Knee wall. An interior wall shortened by the slope of a roofline.

Laminate. Can refer to a material formed by building up layers, as in plywood—or to the process of applying a veneer to a surface, such as a countertop.

Lap joint. Joint formed when one member overlaps another.

Ledger. Horizontal support for an end or edge of an assembly.

Level. Truly horizontal. Also a tool used to determine horizontal.

Miter joint. A joint formed by two pieces cut to the same angle, typically 45 degrees, to create a corner.

Miter joint

Molding. Strips of wood used to cover exposed edges or as decoration.

Nail set. A metal tool used to drive the heads of nails below the surface of wood.

Nominal dimension. The stated size of lumber, such as a 2×4.

On-center (OC). Measurement from the center of one regularly spaced framing member to the next.

Particleboard. Panel comprising wood particles and glue.

Pilot hole. A small hole created to guide a screw or large nail to avoid splitting the wood.

Plywood. Panels formed by laminating layers of wood.

Plumb. Perfectly vertical.

Plumb bob. A weight hung from a string to indicate vertical.

Pressure-treated wood. Lumber or plywood saturated with a solution that makes it resistant to rot and insect damage.

Primer. A coating that seals stains and bonds subsequent coats of paint to a surface.

Pulls. A knob or other form attached to the front of a drawer by which the drawer can be opened.

Rabbet. A notch, typically cut along an edge of one board, to form a joint with a matching notch in another board.

Rabbet

Rails. Horizontal pieces of a cabinet facing.

Rip. To saw wood parallel to its grain pattern.

Router. High-speed power tool that spins steel bits to cut the patterns of moldings and channels.

Scribe. Scratch or otherwise mark.

Sheet goods. Plywood, particleboard, and similar materials produced as panels.

Shim. Wedging thin materials (shims) under or behind surfaces to make them level or plumb.

Spade bit. A drill bit with a cutting blade rather than a long auger twist.

Spackle. A paste that dries and can be sanded after application. It fills cracks and holes in walls.

Square. Surfaces positioned at a 90-degree angle to each other. Also a tool for verifying this.

Stain. A coloring agent, applied like paint, that soaks into the wood rather than coating the surface.

Stile. A vertical member of a door assembly or cabinet facing.

Studs. Regularly spaced vertical framing pieces, such as 2×4s.

Stud finder. Electronic or magnetic tool that locates studs within a finished wall.

Template. A pattern to follow when recreating a precise shape.

Toe kick. Indentation at the bottom of a floor-based cabinet.

Toe nail. To drive a nail diagonally through a corner of a piece of lumber.

Utility knife. A razorlike blade, generally retractable into a handle, for slicing thin materials.

Veneer. A thin surface layer of wood bonded to another material.

METRIC CONVERSIONS

U.S. Units to Metric Equivalents			Metric Units to U.S. Equivalents		
To Convert From	Multiply By	To Get	To Convert From	Multiply By	To Get
Inches	25.4	Millimetres	Millimetres	0.0394	Inches
Inches	2.54	Centimetres	Centimetres	0.3937	Inches
Feet	30.48	Centimetres	Centimetres	0.0328	Feet
Feet	0.3048	Metres	Metres	3.2808	Feet
Yards	0.9144	Metres	Metres	1.0936	Yards
Square inches	6.4516	Square centimetres	Square centimetres	0.1550	Square inches
Square feet	0.0929	Square metres	Square metres	10.764	Square feet
Square yards	0.8361	Square metres	Square metres	1.1960	Square yards
Acres	0.4047	Hectares	Hectares	2.4711	Acres
Cubic inches	16.387	Cubic centimetres	Cubic centimetres	0.0610	Cubic inches
Cubic feet	0.0283	Cubic metres	Cubic metres	35.315	Cubic feet
Cubic feet	28.316	Litres	Litres	0.0353	Cubic feet
Cubic yards	0.7646	Cubic metres	Cubic metres	1.308	Cubic yards
Cubic yards	764.55	Litres	Litres	0.0013	Cubic yards

To convert from degrees Fahrenheit (F) to degrees Celsius (C), first subtract 32, then multiply by ⅝.

To convert from degrees Celsius to degrees Fahrenheit, multiply by ⅘, then add 32.